CROCHET SOCKS THAT ROCK

A beginner's guide to quick
& comfortable crochet socks

ANNA NIKIPIROWICZ

DAVID & CHARLES
—PUBLISHING—

www.davidandcharles.com

DEDICATION

To my sister, Kate, who encouraged
my love of crochet socks.

CONTENTS

CROCHET TECHNIQUES

INTRODUCTION

My introduction to crochet began quite early on, I was taught by my wonderful mum, Lucy, who was the queen of knitted colourwork. I fondly remember watching her speed away with a crochet hook or knitting needles. My whole family was crafty and everyone did something, from macramé to embroidery. Sadly, as a child I did not appreciate the skills I learned and they were quickly forgotten. My beloved mum's passing reignited the desire to crochet and knit again, it was a way of evoking those fond memories. From then on, an obsession was born! I devoured every book available and immersed myself in the designs, colours, yarns and ideas.

My introduction to crochet socks started purely with curiosity. I had been knitting socks for a while, but always thought, why not crochet socks? After experimenting and trying a few patterns a new addiction began!

Crochet socks are amazing! And those who have been following me on social media will know that I cannot stop shouting about them. With so many stunning sock yarn choices on the market, why should the knitters have all the fun? I view socks as a very special make to gift to a loved one. I try to make at least one pair of socks to give to someone special at Christmas. They are a joy to make and I always think – warm feet, warm heart.

This book has really been a dream come true, as I have poured all my love for crochet socks into every page – I have tried to include as much information as I possibly can and I would love everyone to discover the joy of crochet socks.

I hope you enjoy experimenting and making the socks in this book and that your feet will always be adorned in handmade socks.

Anna xx

ABOUT THIS BOOK

This book is divided into two main sections: the first discusses the mechanics of creating crochet socks and includes four basic sock patterns, the second, called The Patterns, contains a series of fully designed and varied sock projects.

THE BASICS

The basic socks are the ideal place to start if you have never crocheted socks before or would just like to start with an uncomplicated sock. You can start simply and then progress onto more advanced socks in the Patterns section.

All the socks are made either cuff down, meaning construction starts at the cuff and ends at the toe, or toe up, meaning construction starts at the toe and ends at the cuff.

HEELS

I have concentrated on four main heel constructions: afterthought heel cuff down; afterthought heel toe up; heel flap cuff down; and short row heel toe up. Each heel has different levels of difficulty with the first two being the easiest and the perfect place to start for a beginner. The last two are more advanced and require a more concentration; however, picture tutorials are provided with the basic sock patterns to guide you through the process.

TOES & CUFFS

Also included is a selection of toes and cuffs that can be used interchangeably. Some are designed for toe up socks, like the toe up ribbing which is used in the Crochet Fair Isle Allover socks, or cuff down, like the ribbing in the Spike Stitch Socks.

Each cuff type has a different hold and fit. If you would like socks to hold well around your ankle, choose ribbing. If you would prefer a softer cuff and you do not want the edge to be tight, choose roll down or picot edge.

Interchanging cuffs depends on which sock construction you have chosen. For example, if you would like to replace the rolled cuff on the Shortie Socks, you could replace it with toe up rib or toe up front and back rib. If you would prefer the Simple Overlay Socks to have a tighter rib, you can simply replace it with cuff down ribbing.

With toes the interchangeability is not that vital, the construction and finished look differ only slightly, mostly producing more square or rounded toes. However, please experiment as you might find that some toe styles easier to work than others.

PATTERNS & TECHNIQUES

In the second half of the book you'll find full crochet patterns for 11 stylish sock designs. The patterns range from straightforward, one-colour socks with simple stitch patterns to eye-catching, textured colour-work socks.

Also in the second half of the book are the Crochet Techniques, which cover all the basic and special skills you need to make the sock projects in this book.

CROCHET TERMINOLOGY

The patterns are all written using US crochet terms. If you are used to working with UK terms, please note the following differences in stitch names:

US TERM	UK TERM
Single crochet	Double crochet
Half double crochet	Half treble crochet
Double crochet	Treble crochet
Treble crochet	Double treble crochet

READING CHARTS

Crochet symbol charts are a visual representation of a written crochet pattern; each stitch has a corresponding symbol. Annotations on the charts indicate row or round numbers and the direction of work. Below are the stitch symbols used for the charts in this book:

←	Rnd direction arrows
()	ch
•	sl st
+	sc
⊹	csc
T	hdc
ↆ	fpdc
⋀	Fan
⋙	C6F

PATTERN ABBREVIATIONS

The following abbreviations have been used in this book:

BLO	back loop only
BPdc	back post double crochet
ch	chain
csc	centre single crochet
C6F	cable 6 front
dc	double crochet
esc	extended single crochet
esc2tog	extended single crochet 2 together
Fan	[2 dc, 2 ch, 2 dc] all in same st or sp
FLO	front loop only
FPdc	front post double crochet
FLdc2d	front loop double crochet 2 down
FPhdc	front post half double crochet
hdc	half double crochet
hdc2tog	half double crochet 2 together
hdc3L	3rd loop half double crochet
hdc3L2tog	half double crochet 2 sts together in 3rd loop
3L	3rd loop
picot	ch3, sl sl in first ch
sc	single crochet
sc2tog	single crochet 2 together
sl st	slip stitch
skip	miss/omit
spike-sc	spike single crochet
st(s)	stitch(es)
rnd(s)	round(s)
RS	right side
WS	wrong side
Yo	yarn over

TOOLS & MATERIALS

All you need to complete the projects in this book are a crochet hook, some sock yarn and a few other simple tools. These pages provide a handy reference guide to choosing those tools and materials.

YARN FIBRE

Yarn can be made from many different natural fibres, such as alpaca and sheep's wool, or from manmade fibres such as acrylic and nylon, all of which come in a range of thicknesses. When choosing yarn for socks there are few factors that must be considered.

WOOL WITH NYLON OR POLYAMIDE

This fibre combination is the most popular for everyday or walking socks. The percentage of nylon or polyamide would usually be 20 to 25%. The wool has wonderful insulation properties, while nylon gives the socks durability, so that your socks can be worn in shoes and be washed with ease.

Wool is often combined with other fibres, such as alpaca or cashmere, or just used as a single element. A tight twist in yarn will mean the yarn is harder wearing, rather than single ply yarn which is much softer and less durable.

There have been lots of sock yarns entering the market that are cotton with nylon or polymide. These yarns are wonderful alternative for anyone allergic to animal fibres or for those who do not wish to use them. These yarns have very little bounce but are hard wearing.

If you are making socks to wear around the house, then any fibre is absolutely fine to use, but do take into account how easy the yarn will be to wash. Constantly hand-washing socks can be tiresome.

WOOL

This very warm fibre is the most popular for crochet. It comes from the fleece of sheep, and different breeds produce different types of wool. For example, Merino sheep produce Merino wool. Other types include Shetland and Botany. Wool yarns are easy to crochet with and have wonderful bounce.

COTTON

This fibre comes in different grades of softness, with Egyptian cotton being the softest. Cotton is a very kind fibre on the skin and suits a lot of people with skin allergies. Cotton shows off stitch definition beautifully, but it can be heavy and less elastic than wool.

MIXED-FIBRE YARNS

There is a vast array of mixed-fibre yarns on the market. They are made by plying different fibres together to produce different textures and weights. They can be natural fibres mixed with synthetic, such as wool and nylon, producing great sock yarn, or all natural, such as mohair and silk or wool and cotton.

YARN WEIGHT

Theoretically you can use any thickness of yarn to crochet socks, the only limitation being whether you would like to wear the socks in shoes or around the house. Crochet stitches are thicker than knit stitches, therefore using thicker yarn will produce bulky socks that might be too thick to comfortably wear in shoes.

Usually, 4ply (fingering) weight yarn is ideal for socks, as it produces light, thin fabric. For socks to wear around the house, 4ply, sport or DK weights are perfect.

In this book, I have used easily available yarn in the following weights: 4ply (fingering) yarn, DK (light worsted) yarn.

YARN COLOUR

There is a vast array of gorgeous sock yarns to choose from, from commercially produced to hand dyed. We really are spoilt for choice. However, there are a few things to consider if you want to achieve lovely stripes or other effects in crochet socks.

Crochet fabric behaves differently to knitted fabric. While knitted fabrics have a lot of stretch widthwise and lengthwise, crochet fabrics tend to stretch more lengthwise than widthwise. This means choosing stitches with a bit more stretch is very important, and this plays a vital role in choosing yarn.

VARIEGATED & SELF-STRIPING YARNS

Let's start with the difference between variegated and self-striping yarns. They are both very similar, apart from one vital difference, variegated yarns have shorter colourways, while the self-striping yarns are dyed with longer changes in between colours. Self-striping yarns will produce consistent stripes, while variegated yarns tend to give you a few colours in a round.

Take West Yorkshire Spinners Signature 4ply, for example, the Passion Fruit Cooler has a lovely long colourway, and depending on which stitches you use for your crochet socks, you are bound to have at least one full round of stripe before the colour changes (1). If you look at Footprints Wool Addicts, it has short changes in colours and will look less uniform, with quick changes. It can look patchy if the stitches are too tall (2).

Crochet stitches vary in height, therefore the effect you will achieve with variegated or self-striping yarns really depends on the crochet stitches your sock pattern uses. The shorter the stitch the less of one colour you will use per stitch, which will result in wider stripes.

Let's go back to the yarn examples: I have used half double stitches and the Passion Fruit Cooler for the basic toe up with afterthought heel socks and the yarn has produced wonderful stripes because it has good length in between colour changes, and I have used medium height stitches (3).

In the basic crochet socks, top down afterthought heel, I have used the variegated Footprints Wool Addicts with single crochet in back loop, the effect is quick burst of colour without any particular order (4).

The biggest joy of working with multicoloured yarns is the effect produced in the colour change. Not only does it keep you interested, but also gives you a unique project. Experiment with different yarns and embrace the unpredictability.

COMMERCIAL & HAND-DYED YARNS

Commercial yarns are produced in vast quantities. They will have a dye lot printed on the label which means that the yarn can be easily matched if you run out. The colour changes or variations are painted by a machine, which makes them more consistent and uniform.

Hand-dyed yarns are independently painted by an artisan. They are usually painted on a base of undyed yarn. The dyes are skillfully applied to the yarn base to create beautiful effects. Independent yarn dyers produce stunning yarns and usually one skein of hand-dyed yarn will be enough to crochet a pair of socks.

SPECKLE YARN

This is one of the most fun types of yarn. The speckles are created by spattering colour on a solid or semi-solid background. Any stitch you use with this yarn will look similar as the yarn has specks of different colours without any particular order. I have used the speckled West Yorkshire Spinners The Croft DK for the shorties socks, which is full of rustic flecks.

GRADIENT YARN

These yarns have colours that gradually fade from one colour to the next, either tonally or into different hues. The change in colour is very subtle in these yarns, which results in very long sections of the same colour.

Gradient yarns are perfect to use with any stitch as you will be able to get few rounds in one colour. I have used these types of yarns in the rib and simple overlay mosaic socks.

SOLID & SEMI-SOLID

Solid yarns are yarns of a single hue throughout, with no variation. They come in a bounty of different colours of varying vibrance and richness.

Semi-solid yarns contain one colour throughout, but unlike solid yarn they also contain a variation of lighter or darker tones within the same colour family. The tonal shifts add depth to the yarn. You can use any stitches with this yarn type. I have used a beautiful semi-solid yarn for the the lace socks.

TOOLS

In addition to yarn, here I've listed all the tools you will need to crochet the patterns in this book.

CROCHET HOOKS

Crochet hooks come in many different types and sizes. They are usually made from steel (for the smallest sizes), aluminium (suitable for most fibres), plastic, wood or bamboo (lightweight and easy on the hands).

I choose my hook depending on which fibre I want to work with, and so that it's easy on my hands. My personal preference is a wooden hook or an aluminium hook with a rubber handle.

The following hook sizes are used throughout this book: 3mm (US C/2 or D/3) and 3.5mm (US E/4).

STITCH MARKERS

Stitch markers are essential in sock making; they are used to mark increases, decreases and to denote the beginning of rounds. I recommend using different coloured markers to make it easy to recognize the beginning of a round and where decreases or increases need to be placed.

Stitch markers need to be easily removable so they can be placed into stitches. There are many removable/hinged markers on the market, including simple ones shaped like safety pins, but unlike standard safety pins they do not have a coil that might snag on yarn.

Stitch markers with lobster clasps are my preference. They come in an array of interesting and fun designs from independent designers.

Split ring stitch markers are also a useful option. The benefits being that they are very easily removable, which makes it ideal when working on small projects such as socks. The only drawback to them is that they can slip off the stitch.

SCISSORS

Sharp scissors are a must for any crocheter. Small embroidery scissors are useful as they have a nice thin, sharp point, which is perfect for snipping yarn on small projects, and they also fit neatly into a project bag. Always cut yarn with scissors, don't try to break it by pulling it, as you might distort your work and hurt your hands.

TAPESTRY NEEDLES

Blunt-tipped needles, such as tapestry or darning needles are essential for weaving in loose yarn ends and sewing up your crochet projects. Make sure that the eye is large enough to thread yarn through. It's best not to use needles that are too fine or sharp, as they will pierce the yarn fibres and split them.

TAPE MEASURE

This is essential for checking tension (gauge) and the length or width of a project. Retractable tape measures are most useful as they fit neatly into your project bag.

WASHI TAPE

Washi tape is perfect for marking your round on charts so that you don't lose your place. Place a strip of washi tape below your round in a Fair Isle chart and above the round you are working on in an overlay mosaic chart, and move it as you work. Placing it below on an overlay mosaic chart will obstruct your view of the previous round, which you need to see when crocheting, as it will determine if you work an sc or an FLdc2d.

PENCIL & PEN

You can use a pencil on a chart or pattern to mark off your rounds. If you plan to scan your pattern or chart and print a copy, then a pen is fine to use.

ANATOMY OF A SOCK

There are different types of sock construction and every sock is made up of several parts. On these pages you'll find a detailed description of the two main sock types and their constituent parts.

HEEL FLAP & GUSSET

These socks are constructed from eight different parts. They will always be made starting from the cuff, which can be worked in rows or rounds.

CUFF

LEG

The leg part of the sock is worked in rounds.

HEEL FLAP

The heel flap is worked in rows as is the heel turn.

FOOT

HEEL TURN

The last two parts of the sock are designed to fit nicely around the heel of your foot. The gusset is created at the point where your foot is largest in circumference and is then decreased to take the stitch count back to the original number.

GUSSET

SOLE

The sole is the bottom part of the foot and that part is worked in rounds.

TOE

AFTERTHOUGHT HEEL & SHORT ROW HEEL

Both of these sock types are made up of six different parts. They can be started either from the toe up or from the cuff down.

The leg or sole is worked in rounds. Very often increases are placed close to the heel to allow for more space around the heel and top of foot. In short-row heel construction, the heel is created as you work. In afterthought construction, an opening is created and the heel is worked after the rest of the sock is completed.

If you are working from the toe up, the leg will be worked in rounds with decreases evenly spaced to take you back to the original number of stitches.

The sock is completed by creation of the cuff either in rounds or rows.

If you are working from the cuff down, the sole and foot will be worked in rounds and decreased to the original number of stitches.

The afterthought construction heel is shaped at the end.

CUFF

LEG

FOOT

HEEL

SOLE

TOE

SIZING YOUR SOCKS

It's important to measure carefully before you make your socks. A snug, well-fitted sock is essential if it's going to be comfortable for wear. Ensuring the perfect fitting socks also includes making a tension swatch. There's more information on tension swatches in Techniques: Tension (gauge).

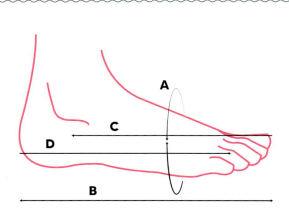

TAKING MEASUREMENTS

A – place tape measure around the widest part of the foot to measure the circumference. Do not pull the tape too tight or too loose.

B – to measure the foot length, place the tape measure from the back of heel to the tip of the longest toe while standing.

C – for toe up socks, measure the foot from the tip of the longest toe to just below the ankle bone while standing. This will determine where to begin the heel.

D – for cuff down socks, measure the foot from the back of the heel to the base of the big toe while standing, this will determine where to start your toe decreases.

NEGATIVE EASE

Negative ease indicates that your crochet piece will be smaller than your actual measurements, resulting in the finished fabric having enough stretch to fit comfortably. It is recommended that you make crochet socks with at least a bit of negative ease to allow for the stretch.

Generally, crochet fabric stretches more lengthwise than widthwise; however, for the patterns in this book, stitches have been used that possess good stretch in both directions.

If you wish, you can make the foot length of socks 2–2.5cm (¾–1in) shorter to allow for better fit around the foot.

You can also customize the sizes, for example, if you wear a shoe size 6 (US 8.5) but wide fit, make the largest size socks with medium size length. If you have a long, narrow foot, make the small/medium size with the largest length. You can always add or take away few rounds to ensure better length.

Tip

All measurements in the book are given in both centimetres and inches; however, I find centimetres more precise than inches because of their smaller increments. I encourage you to give the metric system a try.

CUFFS

Here you will find five methods for working sock cuffs. They are designed for different sock construction, toe up or cuff down. The rib methods have fantastic elasticity and will hold socks up very well. The picot and rolled cuff are purely decorative.

TOE UP FRONT & BACK DC RIB

- Worked over a multiple of 2 stitches.
- Has a slight elasticity and provides a moderate hold.
- Worked in rounds using front and back post stitches.
- Cuff is worked in joined rounds, which means you will sl st as indicated to join each round.

Round 1: ch2 (counts as 1BPdc here and throughout), *1FPdc around next st, 1BPdc around next st; rep from * to end, sl st in top of beg ch to join.

Round 2: ch2, *1FPdc around next st, 1BPdc around next st; rep from * to end, sl st in top of beg ch to join.

Rep last round as many times as desired; three rounds were worked for the sample shown.

Fasten off.

PICOT EDGE CUFF

- Worked over a multiple of 2 stitches.
- This pretty edging gives a charming finish to your socks.
- Provides no elasticity or additional hold.
- This edge is suitable for top down and toe up socks. For top down socks, work the edge into the top of the chainless foundation.
- The Picot edging is worked in joined rounds, which means you will sl st as indicated to join each round.

With RS facing, join yarn with sc to top of the beginning chainless foundation.

Round 1 (RS): ch1, 1sc in every st to end, sl st in first st.

Round 2: ch1, 1sc in first st, picot, * 2sc, picot; rep from * to last st, 1sc, sl st in first st.

Fasten off.

ROLLED EDGE CUFF

- Worked over any number of stitches.
- Results in a very soft edge, perfect for short socks or any edge that requires softness.
- Best worked on toe up socks worked in single crochet in back loop.
- The rolled edge is created by working single crochet in front loop of stitches, this will result in the edge rolling naturally.
- Edge is worked in a continuous spiral, which means you will not need to sl st to join a round or work ch1 at the beginning.

Round 1: 1scFLO in every st to end.

Rep Row 1 for 8 rows, sl st in first st.

Fasten off.

Curl the edge outwards if needed.

CUFF DOWN SC RIBBING

- Worked for an even number of rows.

- Produces a soft and stretchy edge.

- This cuff is worked in in sc rows into the back loop of the stitch and then seamed with slip stitch before it's joined into the row ends for the leg.

Using your colour of choice, make the desired number of chains, taking into account that this will determine the depth of the cuff.

Row 1: 1sc in second ch from hook, 1sc in every ch to end, turn.

Row 2: ch1 (does not count as a st here and throughout), 1scBLO in every st to end, turn.

Rep Row 2 until the required number of rows has been made. (1)

Row 3 (seam cuff): ch1, sl st first and last row of cuff together, working in BLO of each st. Do not fasten off. (2) This might be the same number of rows as stitches, but sometimes more stitches will be worked into the cuff edge to ensure a tighter fit of the cuff.

Row 4: Rotate the piece to work in row ends of cuff. Work ch1, then work the required number of stitches evenly spaced around the top edge of cuff. (3)

Continue onto the leg of the sock as described in the instructions.

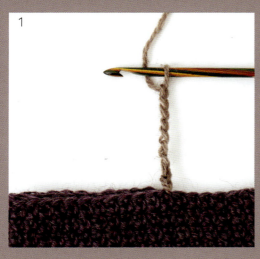

TOE UP SC RIBBING

- Worked over an even number of stitches.

- This is the perfect cuff to work on toe up socks. It can also be worked into any leg edge and provides a soft cuff with good elasticity.

- Worked back and forth in rows in the back loop of every sc and attached to the last rnd of sock using sl sts.

Using your colour of choice, make the desired number of chains, taking into account that this number will determine the depth of the cuff. (1)

Row 1 (RS): 1sc in second ch from hook, 1sc in every ch to end, sl st in next st of last round of sock, turn. (2)

Row 2: ch1, 1scBLO in every st to end, turn. (3)

Row 3: ch1, 1scBLO in every st to end, miss next st of last rnd of sock, sl st in next st, turn.

Row 4: ch1, 1scBLO in every st to end, turn.

Rep rows 3 and 4 until the rib has been worked all around the top of the sock.

Join last row of rib to first row by working sl st through the back of beg chains and back loops only of last row of rib, all the way across. Fasten off.

TOES

There are two main methods for toes, and each has two variations. Top down toes are worked on cuff down socks and the toe up method is used for toe up socks. Both methods are worked in a similar way, the only difference is the placement of increases/decreasess.

TOP DOWN TOE

This toe decrease is suitable for cuff down socks.

There are two ways of working this toe decrease. Both methods are similar but produce slightly different effects. The first one is worked using single crochet, the second using single crochet in the back loop.

Before the toe decreases are worked, the toe needs to be placed in the correct position. To do this, lay the sock flat with the heel at the back, making sure that it's centred. Place a blue marker in the stitch at the side for the beg of round, then count half your total number of foot stitches and place a green marker in this stitch. For example, if you have 40 sts in total, place the blue marker (this will be the first st of the round), then place the green marker in the 20th stitch. You will have 19 sts between markers.

FIRST METHOD

Round 1 (RS): 1sc2tog, 1sc in every st to 2 sts before green marker, 1sc2tog, 1sc in marked st, 1sc2tog, 1sc in every st to 2 sts before blue marker, 1sc2tog, 1sc in marked st. (4 stitches decreased) (1)

Round 2: 1sc in every st to end.

Move the markers up as you work.

Round 3: 1sc2tog, 1sc in every st to 2 sts before green marker, 1sc2tog, 1sc in marked st, 1sc2tog, 1sc in every st to 2 sts before blue marker, 1sc2tog, 1sc in marked st.

Rep Rounds 2 and 3 until desired number of stitches remain. This is usually around 20 stitches. (2)

Remove all markers.

Fasten off leaving a tail of approximately 15cm (6in). Thread the tail onto a tapestry needle and sew the toe opening closed. Weave in the yarn end. (3)

SECOND METHOD

The positioning of the toe and decreases in this method are exactly the same way as for the first method. The differences are that all stitches are worked in single crochet in the back loop only, and the stitches in between the decreases (the ones with the markers) are worked using centre single crochet. This results in a very attractive finished effect.

Using single crochet in back loop only creates fabric with more stretch than standard crochet. (4)

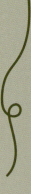

Tip

The construction and finished look of the different toe methods differ only slightly; however, it's well worth experimenting with the techniques because you may find some toe styles easier, or more comfortable, than others.

TOE UP TOE

This method is used for toe up socks. The foundation row is created by working a round of stitches into a chain; placing stitch markers as you go to mark each half of the toe. Increases are worked regularly to expand the toe and provide the correct number of stitches for the foot.

As with the top down toe, there are two ways of working this. The only difference is the placement of increases, which results in slightly rounder toe in the first method.

FIRST METHOD

Make desired number of chains (this will be the width of the top of the toes). Usually, this number is 11 or 13 chains for 4ply and DK yarns.

Round 1: 3sc in 2nd ch from hook, place green marker in the centre sc of 3-sc group, 1sc in each ch to last ch, 3sc in next ch, place blue marker in the centre sc of 3-sc group, working into opposite side of foundation chain, 1sc in each ch to end. Move the markers up as you work. (1)

Also note that your new round will start 1 st before the green marker.

Round 2: 2sc in next st, 1sc in st with green marker, 2sc in next st, 1sc in each st to 1 st before blue marker, 2sc in next st, 1sc in st with blue marker, 2sc in next st, 1sc in every st to 1 st before green marker.

Round 3: 1sc in each st to end, moving markers as you work.

Round 4: 2sc in next st, 1sc in st with green marker, 2sc in next st, 1sc in each st to 1 st before blue marker, 2sc in next st, 1sc in st with blue marker, 2sc in next st, 1sc in every st to 1 st before green marker.

Rep Rounds 3 and 4 until desired number of stitches is reached. (2)

SECOND METHOD

The difference between this method and the first is in the set up and placement of the increases.

Make the desired number of chains (this will determine the width of the top of the toes). Usually this number is between 11 and 13 chains for 4ply and DK yarns.

Round 1: 1sc in 2nd ch from hook (place green marker in st just made), 1sc in each ch across, working into opposite side of foundation chain, 1sc (place blue marker in st just made), sc in each ch across.

Round 2: 3sc in first st (move green marker to centre sc of 3-sc group), sc in each st to blue marker, 3sc in marked st (move blue marker to centre sc of 3-sc group), sc in each st to end.

Round 3: 1sc in each st to end, moving the markers up as you work.

Round 4: 1sc in each st to green marker, 3sc in marked st (moving marker up to middle sc of 3-sc group just made), 1sc in each st to blue marker, 3sc in marked st (moving marker up to middle sc of 3-sc group just made), 1sc in each st to end.

Round 5: 1sc in each st to end.

Rep Rounds 4 and 5 until desired number of stitches is reached. (3 shown sideways and 4)

Tip

When working the first method, the chains where the first 3sc groups are placed can stretch and create a hole. To avoid this, work into the back bumps of the chain on the first half of foundation chain, then into the two strands of chain on the second half.

HEELS

There are things to consider when choosing a heel type for socks: a heel flap provides durability and comfort; afterthought heels are easy to make and are perfect for lace or colourwork socks; a short row heel offers a snug fit and, as with the heel flap, is seamless.

CUFF DOWN, HEEL FLAP

TURNING THE HEEL

Once you have worked the leg and heel flap of your sock, it's time to turn the heel.

Row 1: ch1, and work as many stitches as instructed, 1sc2tog, 1sc in next st, turn, leaving rem sts unworked.

Row 2: ch1, 2sc, 1sc2tog, 1sc in next st, turn. You will have equal amount of stitches left unworked on each side. (1)

Row 3: ch1, 1sc in each st to 1 st from end of row, 1sc2tog working the first half of the st in the next st and the second half into the next st 2 rows below, 1sc, turn. (2 and 3)

You can see where the sc2tog and 1sc has been worked. Rep Row 3 as many times as instructed

You have now completed the heel turn. (4)

GUSSET

Round 1 (RS): ch1, work each sc across heel. (5)

Round 2: work as many sc as instructed along edge of heel flap, place blue marker on the last st. (6)

Round 3: 1esc in every st of foot. (7)

Round 4: work as many sc as instructed along edge of heel flap, place yellow marker on the first st made. (8)

You are now back at the end of rnd.

Start gusset decreasing as instructed in the pattern for basic socks with heel flap.

After all stitches are decreased on gusset, your work should look like this (9)

sc2tog over these two sts

sc2tog

1sc

sc2tog

CUFF DOWN, AFTERTHOUGHT HEEL

HEEL OPENING

Work to the point in the pattern where the heel needs to be placed. (1)

Work instructed number of chainless foundation single crochet. (2)

Skip half the number of stitches on main piece, then work in scBLO to end. (3)

AFTERTHOUGHT HEEL

With RS facing, join yarn with 1sc at the bottom right corner of the heel opening, working along the sole, work indicated number of sts into underside of chainless foundation. Place blue marker in last st. (4)

Work instructed number of stitches on the leg part. Place green marker in ast st. (5)

Work decreases as indicated until a small opening is left. Sew up to close. (6)

TOE UP, AFTERTHOUGHT HEEL

HEEL OPENING

Work to point in the pattern where heel needs to be placed.

Work instructed number of chainless foundation single crochet. (1)

Skip half the number of stitches on main piece, then work in hdc to end. **(2)**

AFTERTHOUGHT HEEL

With RS facing, join yarn with 1sc at the bottom right corner of the heel opening, working along the sole, work indicated number of sts, place blue marker in last st. (3)

Work instructed number of stitches on the other side of chainless foundation. Place green marker in last st. (4)

Work decreases as indicated until a small opening is left. Sew up to close. (5)

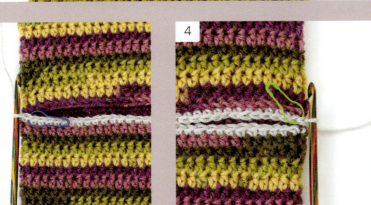

TOE UP, SHORT ROW HEEL

For the heel, you will work in rows over half the number of stitches.

Keep marker in place to ensure you work the heel in the correct position relative to the toe and work the following rows of pattern:

Row 1 (RS): work sc in each st of half the number of sts of sock, turn.

Row 2 (WS): ch1 (does not count as a st), work across sts of last row, leaving the last st unworked, turn.

Row 3: ch1, 1sc in every st to 1 st before end, leave rem st unworked, turn.

Rep Row 3 as many times as instructed, ending with WS facing for next row.

When the above rows are done, the heel should look like this. The first half of the heel is completed. (1)

Now, we will work into the sides of the steps and slip stitch into the sc we have missed at the end of each row.

Next row (WS): ch1, 1sc in each st to end, 1sc in side of row below, 1sl st in missed st from row below, turn. (2)

1

2

sc inside of sc

sl st

To work the sc into side of row below: Insert your hook into the side of sc from previous row, picking up the two strands of the st. Work sc as normal. Now, sl st into the missed sc. (3)

When you work the next row, you can see how the heel rounds up and will eventually form a cup. Continue, repeating the steps above to work all the missed stitches. (4)

Basic Sock #1
CUFF DOWN, HEEL FLAP

MATERIALS

John Arbon Textiles Exmoor Sock 4ply (60% Exmoor Blueface, 20% Corriedale, 10% Zwartbles, 10% nylon), 200m (218¾yd) in 50g (1¾oz) skein (hank), in the following shades:

- A – Bell Heather x 1 skein (hank)
- B – Fairy Thimble x 2 skeins (hanks)

3mm (US C/2 or D/3) crochet hook (or size required to match tension [gauge])

3 x different colour lockable stitch markers (I will be using green, red and yellow)

TENSION (GAUGE)

After steam blocking: 13 sts and 10 rounds measure 5 x 5cm (2 x 2in) over esc worked in the round using a 3mm (US C/2 or D/3) hook. When you are making your tension swatch make sure it is worked in the round as your tension can differ between working in rows and rounds.

FINISHED SIZE

After steam blocking: Leg (measured from top of heel to top of cuff) 12cm (4¾in) in length.

SOCK SIZE	S	M	L
Shoe size UK (US)	3-4 (5-6)	5-6 (7-8)	7-8 (9-10)
Foot circumference (approximate)	15.5cm (6in)	17cm (6¾in)	18.5cm (7¼in)
Foot length (approximate)	19.5cm (7¾in)	21cm (8¼in)	22.5cm (8¾in)

Pattern Note

Please note that the size measurements listed here were taken after steam blocking and that the crochet fabric might stretch more lengthwise and widthwise with wet blocking.

SOCK CONSTRUCTION

The heel of this sock is structured around a heel flap, heel turn and gusset, which creates ample space around the heel and the top of the foot, resulting in a perfectly fitting sock.

The socks are started at the cuff rib, which is worked in rows then seamed. Extended single crochet stitches for the leg are worked into the edge of the cuff.

Next, you will work the heel flap, heel turn, then the gusset decreases.

Finally, the toe decreases are worked before finishing with the seaming of the toe opening.

SOCKS (MAKE 2)

CUFF

Using a 3mm (US C/2 or D/3) hook and yarn A, ch11 (11) (11).

Row 1 (RS): 1sc in 2nd ch from hook, 1sc in every ch, turn. 10 (10) (10) sts

Row 2: ch1 (does not count as a st here and throughout), 1scBLO in every st, turn.

Rep Row 2 a further 38 (42) (46) times, ending with WS facing for the next row.

SEAM CUFF

Hold first and last rows together and, work in BLO of sts of both rows to join, ch1, sl st across. Do not fasten off.

LEG

Rotate piece to work in row-ends of cuff.

Next round: ch1, 40 (44) (48) esc (1 st into edge of each row). Do not join.

Place yellow marker in first st for beginning of rnd and move marker up as you work.

Break off yarn A and join yarn B.

Continue to work esc in a continuous spiral until work measures 11cm (4¼in).

HEEL FLAP

For the heel flap you will work back and forth in rows of sc over half the sock, leaving the rem (top of the foot) sts unworked.

Row 1 (RS): 20 (22) (24) sc, leave rem sts unworked, turn.

Row 2: ch1, 1sc in each st to end of row, turn. 20 (22) (24) sts

Rep Row 2 a further 16, (18, 20) times. Total of 18, (20, 22) rows worked on the heel flap.

HEEL TURN

Row 1: ch1, 10 (11) (12) sc, 1sc2tog, 1sc in next st, leave rem sts unworked, turn. 12 (13) (14) sts

Row 2: ch1, 2sc, 1sc2tog, 1sc in next st, turn. 4 (4) (4) sts

Row 3: ch1, 3sc, 1sc2tog working the first half of the decrease in the next st and the second half into the next st 2 rows below, 1sc, turn. 5 (5) (5) sts

Row 4: ch1, 1sc in each st to 1 st from end of row, 1sc2tog working the first half of the st in the next st and the second half into the next st 2 rows below, 1sc, turn. 6 (6) (6) sts

Rep Row 4 a further 4 (6) (6) times. 10 (12) (12) sts

SIZE S AND L ONLY

Next row: ch1, 1sc in each st to 1 st from end of row, 1sc2tog working the first half of the st in the next st and the second half into the next st 2 rows below, turn.

Rep last row once more. 10 (12) (12) sts

All the unworked stitches have been used up and you have turned your heel.

ALL SIZES: GUSSET

Round 1 (RS): ch1, 10 (12) (12) sc of heel, 10 (11) (12) sc evenly along edge of heel flap (working 1 st in every other row, approx.), place blue marker on last st made, 1esc in next 20, (22, 24) sts of foot, 10 (11) (12) sc evenly along edge of heel flap, place green marker on first st st made. 50 (56) (64) sts

You are now at the end of the rnd.

Start working in a continuous spiral in esc. Place yellow marker into the next st (first st of Rnd 2) to denote the beg of rnd.

Move all markers up as you work.

Round 2: 1esc in every st to 2 sts before blue marker, 1esc2tog, 1esc in marked st, 1esc in every st to green marker, 1esc in marked st, 1esc2tog, 1esc in every st to end. 48 (54) (62) sts

Round 3: 1esc in every st to end.

FOOT

You can now remove all markers and work in esc in a continuous spiral until work measures 15.5 (17) (18.5)cm/6 (6¾) (7¼)in from the back of the heel.

TOE

Break off yarn B and join yarn A

Lay the sock flat with the heel at the back and sole facing upwards, making sure that it's centred. Place blue marker in the st at the right-hand side of the sock on the 'fold' (you may need to undo or work few stitches to reach this point). This marks the beg of rnd.

The toe is worked in sc in a continuous spiral. Start Rnd 1 in the st immediately after the stitch with blue marker.

Round 1: 1sc2tog, 15 (17) (19) sc, 1sc2tog, 1sc in next st, place green marker in st just made, 1sc2tog, 1sc in every st to 2 sts before blue marker, 1sc2tog, 1sc in marked st. 36 (40) (44) sts

Round 2: 1sc in every st to end, moving markers up as you work.

Round 3: 1sc2tog, 1sc in every st to 2 sts before green marker, 1sc2tog, 1sc in marked st, 1sc2tog, 1sc in every st to 2 sts before blue marker, 1sc2tog, 1sc in marked st. 32 (36) (40) sts

Rep Rounds 2 and 3 a further 3 (4) (5) times. 20 (20) (20) sts

Fasten off leaving a tail approximately 15cm/6in in length. Thread yarn tail onto tapestry needle and sew toe opening closed. Weave in the end.

MAKING UP

Weave in the ends.

When you complete your socks, you may wish to wet block them. To do this, soak them in lukewarm water, squeeze out excess moisture and pin out to size or place them on sock blockers. I pin them out on the side and in line with the sides of toes and heel. Allow to dry naturally.

Alternatively, you can steam block your socks, by pinning them out and steaming with an iron, taking care that the hot iron does not touch the fabric.

Basic Sock #2
CUFF DOWN, AFTERTHOUGHT HEEL

MATERIALS

Langyarns Wool Addicts Footprints (45% cotton, 42% virgin wool, 13% polyamide), 4ply, 400m (437½yd) in a 100g (3½oz) ball, in the following shade:

• A – Multicolour (0002) x 1 ball

West Yorkshire Spinners Signature 4ply (75% wool, 25% nylon), 4ply, 400m (437½yd) in a 100g (3½oz) ball, in the following shade:

• B – Marshmallow (0011) x 1 ball

3mm (US C/2 or D/3) crochet hook (or size required to match tension [gauge])

2 x different colour lockable stitch markers (I will be using green, blue and yellow)

TENSION (GAUGE)

After steam blocking: 11 sts and 12 rounds measure 5 x 5cm (2 x 2in) over scBLO worked in the round using a 3mm (US C/2 or D/3) hook. When you are making your tension swatch make sure it is worked in the round as your tension can differ between working in rows and rounds.

FINISHED SIZE

After steam blocking: Leg (measured from top of heel to top of picot edge) 9cm (3½in) in length.

SOCK SIZE	S	M	L
Shoe size UK (US)	3–4 (5–6)	5–6 (7–8)	7–8 (9–10)
Foot circumference (approximate)	17.5cm (7in)	19cm (7½in)	20.5cm (8in)
Foot length (approximate)	21cm (8¼in)	23cm (9in)	25cm (10in)

Pattern Note

Please note that the size measurements listed here were taken after steam blocking and that the crochet fabric might stretch more lengthwise and widthwise with wet blocking.

SOCK CONSTRUCTION

This sock is made by working single crochet in the back loop only, which creates a nice, stretchy fabric.

The sock starts with chainless foundation, which provides a stretchy, soft top edge of the sock. Increases on the leg create room for the heel.

The opening for the afterthought heel is created with chainless foundation single crochet. Decreases after the heel opening take the stitch count back to the original number.

Toe and heel are worked in back loop single crochet, with centre single crochet placed between the decreases. This creates an interesting decorative effect.

The picot cuff is worked into the intial chainless foundation.

SOCKS (MAKE 2)

CUFF AND LEG

Using a 3mm (US C/2 or D/3) hook and yarn A, create 40 (44) (48) chainless foundation sc, join with sl st to form a loop.

Place a yellow marker to indicate the beg of round. Move marker up as you work.

Round 1 (RS): ch1 (does not count as a st), 1scBLO in every st to end.

Rounds 2 and 3: 1scBLO in every st to end.

Round 4: [2scBLO in the next st, 19 (21) (23) scBLO] twice. 42 (46) (50) sts

Rounds 5 to 9: 1scBLO in every st to end.

Round 10: [2scBLO in the next st, 20 (22) (24) scBLO] twice. 44 (48) (52) sts

Rounds 11 to 15: 1scBLO in every st to end.

Round 16: [2scBLO in the next st, 21 (23) (25) scBLO] twice. 46 (50) (54) sts

Rounds 17 and 18: 1dcBLO in every st to end.

SEPARATING FOR HEEL

Round 19: Chainless foundation 23 (25) (27) sc, skip next 23 (25) (27) sts, 1scBLO in every st to end.

Round 21: 23 (25) (27) scBLO across foundation sts, 1scBLO in every st to end.

Rounds 21 and 22: 1scBLO in every st to end.

Round 23: [1sc2togBLO, 21 (23) (25) scBLO] twice. 44 (48) (52) sts

Rounds 24 to 28: 1scBLO in every st to end.

Round 29: [1sc2togBLO, 20, (22), (24) scBLO] twice. 42 (46) (50) sts

Rounds 30 to 34: 1scBLO in every st to end.

Round 35: [1sc2togBLO, 19, (21), (23) scBLO] twice. 40 (44) (48) sts

The marker can now be removed.

Work 8 (13) (18) rounds in scBLO, or until foot measures 11 (13) (15)cm/4¼ (5) (6)in from heel opening.

Fasten off.

TOES

Lay the sock flat with the heel opening at the back, making sure that it's centred. Place the blue stitch marker on the side of the top of the sock, this will be your beg of round.

Change to yarn B.

Round 1: 1sc2togBLO, 15 (17) (19) scBLO, 1sc2togBLO, 1sc, place green marker in st just made, 1sc2togBLO, 1scBLO in every st to 2 sts before blue marker, 1sc2togBLO, 1sc in marked st. 36 (40) (44) sts

Round 2: 1scBLO in every st to green marker, 1csc in marked st, 1scBLO in every st to blue marker, 1csc in marked st.

Round 3: 1sc2togBLO, 1scBLO in every st to 2 sts before green marker, 1sc2togBLO, 1csc in marked st, 1sc2togBLO, 1scBLO in every st to 2 sts before blue marker, 1sc2tog BLO, 1csc in marked st. 32 (36) (40) sts

Rep Rounds 2 and 3 another 3 (4) (5) more times. 20 sts

Fasten off leaving a tail of approximately 15cm (6in). Using a tapestry needle and the yarn tail, sew the toe opening closed. Weave in the yarn end.

AFTERTHOUGHT HEEL

The heel is worked in a continuous spiral. Extra stitches are worked around the heel opening to help prevent any holes at the point where you separated for the heel.

With RS facing, join B with 1sc at the bottom right corner of the heel opening. Working along the sole, work 25 (27) (29) scBLO evenly spaced, place blue marker on last st, working along the underside of foundation chain. Work 25, (27) (29) scBLO evenly spaced along the leg part, place green marker in last st. 50 (54) (58) sts

Round 1: 1sc2togBLO, 1scBLO in every st to 2 sts before blue marker, 1sc2togBLO, 1csc in marked st, 1sc2togBLO, 1scBLO in every st to 2 sts before green marker, 1sc2togBLO, 1csc in marked st. 46 (50) (54) sts

Round 2: 1scBLO in every st to blue marker, 1csc in marked st, 1scBLO in every st to green marker, 1csc in marked st.

Round 3: 1sc2togBLO, 1scBLO in every st to 2 sts before blue marker, 1sc2togBLO, 1csc in marked st, 1sc2togBLO, 1scBLO in every st to 2 sts before green marker, 1sc2togBLO, 1csc in marked st. 42 (46) (50) sts

Rep Rounds 2 and 3 another 5 (5) (5) more times. 22 (26) (30) sts

Fasten off leaving a tail approximately 15cm (6in) in length. Using a tapestry needle and the yarn tail, sew the heel opening closed. Weave in the yarn end.

PICOT CUFF

With RS facing, join B in any st of the beginning chainless foundation sc.

Round 1 (RS): ch1, 1sc in every st to end, sl st in first st to join. 40 (44) (48) sts

Round 2: ch1, 1sc, picot, [2sc, picot] to last st, 1sc, sl st in first st to join.

Fasten off.

MAKING UP

Weave in the ends.

When you complete your socks, you may wish to wet block them. To do this soak your socks in lukewarm water, squeeze out excess moisture and pin out to size or place them on sock blockers. I pin them out on the side and in line with the sides of toes and heel. Allow to dry naturally.

Alternatively, you can steam block your socks by pinning them out and steaming with an iron, taking care that the hot iron does not touch the fabric.

Basic Sock #3
TOE UP, AFTERTHOUGHT HEEL

MATERIALS

West Yorkshire Spinners Signature 4ply (75% wool, 25% nylon), 4ply, 400m (437½yd) in a 100g (3½oz) ball, in the following shades:

- A – Dusty Miller (0129) x 1 ball
- B – Passion Fruit Cooler (0611) x 1 ball

3mm (US C/2 or D/3) crochet hook (or size required to match tension [gauge])

2 x different colour lockable stitch markers (I will be using green and blue)

TENSION (GAUGE)

After steam blocking: 13 sts and 9 rounds measure 5 x 5cm (2 x 2in) over hdc worked in the round using a 3mm (US C/2 or D/3) hook. When you are making your tension swatch make sure it is worked in the round as your tension can differ between working in rows and rounds.

FINISHED SIZE

After steam blocking: Leg (measured from chainless foundation made when separating for heel, to top of cuff) 11cm (4¼in) in length.

SOCK SIZE	S	M	L
Shoe size UK (US)	3-4 (5-6)	5-6 (7-8)	7-8 (9-10)
Foot circumference (approximate)	16.5cm (6½in)	18cm (7in)	19.5cm (7¾in)
Foot length (approximate)	20cm (7¾in)	22cm (8¾in)	24cm (9½in)

Pattern Note

Please note that the size measurements listed here were taken after steam blocking and that the crochet fabric might stretch more lengthwise and widthwise with wet blocking.

SOCK CONSTRUCTION

This sock pattern is perfect for beginners because it has the easiest construction. It's worked from the toe up in single crochet in a continuous spiral. The increases of the toe start immediately on the first round, which results in a more rounded toe.

The foot and the leg are worked in half double crochet, which creates a slightly looser fabric.

When the foot is complete, an opening for the afterthought heel is created by working chainless foundation single crochet. This creates a lovely, soft edge.

The cuff is worked perpendicular to the leg, back and forth in rows in back loop single crochet, joined to the last round of the leg with slip stitches.

The afterthought heel is worked in a continuous spiral around the heel opening, decreasing until a small opening is left, which can be sewn up.

SOCKS (MAKE 2)

TOE

Using a 3mm (US C/2 or D/3) hook and yarn A, ch11 (11) (11).

Round 1 (RS): 3sc in 2nd ch from hook, place green marker in the centre sc of 3-sc group, 8sc, 3sc in next ch, place blue marker in the centre sc of 3-sc group, working into opposite side of foundation chain, 8sc. 22 (22) (22) sts

Move the stitch markers up as you work.

Also note that your new round will start 1 st before the green marker.

Round 2: 2sc in next st, 1sc in st with green marker, 2sc in next st, 1sc in each st to 1 st before blue marker, 2sc in next st, 1sc in st with blue marker, 2sc in next st, 1sc in every st to 1 st before green marker. 26 (26) (26) sts

Round 3: 1sc in each st to end, moving markers up as you work.

Round 4: 2sc in next st, 1sc in st with green marker, 2sc in next st, 1sc in each st to 1 st before blue marker, 2sc in next st, 1sc in st with blue marker, 2sc in next st, 1sc in every st to 1 st before green marker. 30 (30) (30) sts

Rep Rounds 3 and 4 a further 3 (4) (5) times. 42 (46) (50) sts

FOOT

Work 1hdc in next st and 1hdc in st with green marker.

Change to yarn B.

All markers can now be removed.

Work in hdc in a continuous spiral until sock measures 16 (17) (18)cm/6¼ (6¾) (7)in, or until it comes to your ankle bone, or is 5cm (2in) shorter than the length of your foot. There are different ways to gauge this, but one of the best reasons for making toe up socks is that you can try them on as you work to ensure a perfect fit. If you are making them as a gift, then just go with the measurements above.

Place your toe flat and in line with the sock so that the start of next the part is done exactly at the right point. You may need to work a few more sts or unravel a few sts so that your hook is at the side of your sock.

SEPARATING FOR HEEL

Round 1: chainless foundation 21 (23) (25) sc, skip next 21 (23) (25) sts, 1hdc in every st to end.

Round 2: 21 (23) (25) hdc across foundation sts, 1hdc in every st to end. 42 (46) (50) sts

LEG

Work in hdc in a continuous spiral for 14 more rounds. Sl st to first st.

CUFF

The cuff is worked perpendicular to the leg, back and forth in rows in back loop single crochet, and joined to the last round of sock with sl sts.

Change to yarn A.

Ch 7 (7) (7).

Row 1 (RS): 1sc in second ch from hook, 5sc, skip next st of last round of sock, sl st in next st, turn. 6 (6) (6) sts

Row 2: ch1 (does not count as a st), 1scBLO in every st, turn.

Row 3: ch1, 1scBLO in every st, skip next st with sl st and next st of last round of sock, sl st in next st, turn.

Row 4: ch1, 1scBLO in every st to end, turn.

Rep Rows 3 and 4, until the rib has been worked all around the top of sock.

Join last row of rib to first row by sl st across row, working into back of beg chains of row 1 and BLO of last row of rib.

Fasten off.

AFTERTHOUGHT HEEL

The heel is worked in a continuous spiral. Note that extra stitches are worked around the heel opening to help prevent any holes at the point where you separated for the heel.

With RS facing, join yarn A with 1sc at the bottom right corner of heel opening. Working along the sole, make 23 (25) (27) sc evenly spaced, place blue marker in last st made, working along underside of foundation ch, work 23 (25) (27) sc evenly spaced, place green marker in last st made. 46 (50) (54) sts

Move markers up as you work.

Round 1: 1sc2tog, 1sc in every st to 2 sts before blue marker, 1sc2tog, 1sc in marked st, 1sc2tog, 1sc in every st to 2 sts before green marker, 1sc2tog, 1sc in marked st. 44 (46) (48) sts

Round 2: 1sc in each st to end.

Round 3: 1sc2tog, 1sc in every st to 2 sts before blue marker, 1sc2tog, 1sc in marked st, 1sc2tog, 1sc in every st to 2 sts before green marker, 1sc2tog, 1sc in marked st. 40 (42) (44) sts

Rep Rounds 2 and 3 a further 7 (7) (7) times. 20 (22) (24) sts

Fasten off leaving a tail approximately 15cm (6in) in length. Using a tapestry needle and yarn tail, sew the heel opening closed. Weave in the yarn end.

MAKING UP

Weave in the ends.

When you complete your socks, you may wish to wet block them. To do this soak your socks in lukewarm water, squeeze out excess moisture and pin out to size or place them on sock blockers. I pin them out on the side and in line with the sides of toes and heel. Allow to dry naturally.

Alternatively, you can steam block your socks by pinning them out and steaming with an iron, taking care that the hot iron does not touch the fabric.

Basic Sock #4
TOE UP, SHORT ROW HEEL

MATERIALS

Rowan Sock (75% wool, 25% polyamide), 4ply, 400m (437½yd) in a 100g (3½oz) ball, in the following shade:

- Ash (012) x 1 ball

3mm (US C/2 or D/3) crochet hook (or size required to match tension [gauge])

2 x different colour lockable stitch markers (I will be using green and blue)

TENSION (GAUGE)

After steam blocking: 12 sts and 9 rnds measure 5 x 5cm (2 x 2in) over esc worked in the round using a 3mm hook (US C/2 or D/3). When you are making your tension swatch make sure it is worked in the round as your tension can differ between working in rows and rounds.

FINISHED SIZE

After steam blocking: Leg (measured from top of heel to top of cuff) 8cm (3in) in length.

SOCK SIZE	S	M	L
Shoe size UK (US)	3-4 (5-6)	5-6 (7-8)	7-8 (9-10)
Foot circumference (approximate)	16.5cm (6½in)	18cm (7in)	20cm (8in)
Foot length (approximate)	20cm (8in)	22cm (8¾in)	24cm (9½in)

Pattern Note

Please note that the size measurements listed here were taken after steam blocking and that the crochet fabric might stretch more lengthwise and widthwise with wet blocking.

SOCK CONSTRUCTION

This sock is started at the toe, which is worked in single crochet in the round, in a continuous spiral. The foot is also worked in a continuous spiral, using extended single crochet. When you work in a continuous spiral, it is vital to use a stitch marker to keep track of the beginning of the round.

Increases are worked before the heel to provide more room for the heel and top of foot. The heel is worked back and forth in rows using single crochet. The leg is worked in the round and includes decreases to take the stitch count back to the original number.

The cuff is worked in joined rounds, using front and back post double crochet stitches.

SOCKS (MAKE 2)

TOE

Using a 3mm (US C/2 or D/3) hook, ch13 (13) (13).

Round 1 (RS): 1sc in 2nd ch from hook and in each ch across, rotate to work into opposite side of foundation chain, sc in each ch across, do not join round. 24 (24) (24) sts

Round 2: 3sc in first st (place green marker in centre sc of 3-sc group), 11sc, 3sc in next st (place blue marker in centre sc of 3-sc group), 11sc. 28 (28) (28) sts

Note that the round starts at green marker.

Move markers up as you work.

Round 3: 1sc in each st to end.

Round 4: 1sc in each st to green marker, 3sc in marked st, moving marker up to centre sc of 3-sc group just made, sc around to next marker, 3sc in marked st, moving marker up to centre sc of 3-sc group just made, sc to end. 32 (32) (32) sts

Round 5: 1sc in each st to end.

Rep Rounds 4 and 5 another 2 (3) (4) times. 40 (44) (48) sts

FOOT

The blue marker can now be removed, keeping only the green marker in place to indicate the beginning of round.

Work in esc in a continuous spiral, moving marker up as you work, for 21 rnds or until sock measures 14 (15) (16) cm/5½ (6) (6¼)in.

Next round: 2esc in next st, 19 (21) (23) esc, 2esc in next st, esc to end. 42 (46) (50) sts

Work 2 rounds in esc.

Next round: 2esc in next st, 20 (22) (23) esc, 2esc in next st, esc to end. 44, (48, 52 sts).

Work 1 round in esc.

HEEL

Heel is worked in rows over half of the total number of stitches.

Keep green marker in place to ensure you work the heel in the correct position relative to the toe.

Row 1 (RS): 22 (24) (26) sc, turn.

Row 2 (WS): ch1 (does not count as a st), 21 (23) (25) sc, leave rem st unworked, turn. 21 (23) (25) sts

Row 3: ch1, 1sc in every st to 1 st before end, leave rem st unworked, turn. 20 (22) (24) sts

Rep row 3 another (10 (10) (12) more times, ending with WS facing for next row. 10 (12) (12) sts

Next row (WS): ch1, 1sc in each st to end, 1sc in side of row below, 1sl st in missed st from row below, turn. 11, (13) (13) sts

Next row (RS): ch1, miss sl st, sc in each st to end, 1sc in side of row below, sl st in missed st from row below, turn. 12 (14) (14) sts

Rep last row 9 (10) (12) more times. Do not turn after last row. 22 (24) (26) sts

1esc in each st to marker.

The heel should be parallel to the toe.

LEG

You will now return to working esc in the round, in a continuous spiral. Move marker up as you work.

Rounds 1 to 3: 1esc in each st to end.

Round 4: 1esc2tog, 20 (22) (24) esc, 1esc2tog, esc in each st to end. 42 (46) (50) sts

Rounds 5 to 7: 1esc in each st to end.

Round 8: 1esc2tog, 19 (21) (23) esc, 1esc2tog, esc in each st to end. 40 (44) (48) sts

Rounds 9 to 11: 1esc in each st to end.

CUFF

Cuff is worked in joined rounds. Join each round with a sl st in first st.

You can remove the marker now.

Round 1: ch2 (counts as 1BPdc here and throughout), [1FPdc around next st, 1BPdc around next st] to end, sl st into beg ch1 to join.

Round 2: ch2, [1FPdc, 1BPdc] to end, sl st to top of ch3 from the beginning of round.

Rep Round 2 twice more.

Fasten off.

MAKING UP

Weave in the ends.

When you complete your socks, you may wish to wet block them. To do this soak your socks in lukewarm water, squeeze out excess moisture and pin out to size or place them on sock blockers. I pin them out on the side and in line with the sides of toes and heel. Allow to dry naturally.

Alternatively, you can steam block your socks by pinning them out and steaming with an iron, taking care that the hot iron does not touch the fabric.

CUSTOMIZING SOCKS

One of the most wonderful attributes of handmade items is that we can adapt them to fit us. Here I will explain how you can customize your socks to fit your feet whatever the length or width.

Trying Socks On

Crochet fabric is not as elastic as knit fabric. Crochet socks will stretch when you try them on. To restore the shape, squeeze the socks gently in your hands.

When trying on socks, do not pull them on from the cuff, but ease them gradually onto your foot. Push the toe part so it encloses your toes nicely with the seam laying on top of your toes.

The simplest way to customize socks is to change yarn and hook size – if you would like smaller socks, switch to a smaller hook, if you would like bigger ones, use a larger hook. If you want just slightly bigger socks, switching to a thicker yarn will probably be enough; however, sometimes changes will need to be made to the pattern.

Most of the socks in this book are designed in three sizes; however, some, such as the Lace Socks, only come in two sizes due to the length of the pattern repeat. The Pine Tree socks only have one size because of the number of stitches in the colourwork chart – adding or taking away another repeat would make the socks too large or too small.

Most of the sock patterns in this book include a pattern repeat consisting of 2 or 4 stitches, which makes them ideal for resizing.

Adjusting the number of stitches in socks is very manageable and nothing at all to be scared of. All you have to think about is that the stitch count has to be divisable by 2, and always increase or decrease by 4 stitches.

If you wish to resize, start with the basic socks; I will give you examples of how to calculate new stitch numbers overleaf.

HEEL FLAP & GUSSET SOCKS

The largest size in the basic socks has 48 sts. Let's say, for example, that we would like to make them wider by 4 more stitches, that will be 52 sts.

The cuff is very simple, just work 2 or 4 more rows, then work 52 sts into the edges.

The leg is worked in a continuous spiral and you can make it to the length you desire. Bear in mind that if you wish to make the leg part longer, you must start with more stitches, then decrease before you reach the heel flap.

The heel flap is worked on half of the number of stitches: 52 divided by 2 = 26, the 26 sts are worked in single crochet and the remaining stitches of the sock are left unworked for the time being. Because crochet stitches are taller than they are wide, the heel flap has 2 rows less than the number of stitches: we have 26 sts, so we will work 24 rows. However, if you have low instep you might wish to make the heel flap shorter by 2 or 4 rows.

The heel turn is also worked in rows on approximately 60% of the stitches of the heel flap.

1sc in half the number of stitches + sc2tog + 1sc = 60%, so that is in stitches 26 divided by 2 = 13 + sc2tog + 1sc = 15 sts. Turn the heel as normal making sure all the stitches have been worked.

Work the stitches for the gusset by working 1sc in every other row of the heel flap, you can add additional stitches if you wish to avoid any gaps. Set up the gusset decreases as given in the pattern, including the extra stitches, decrease until you have the original number of stitches and continue onto foot.

When you are ready to shape the toes, position a stitch marker to denote the beginning of the round (as in the pattern). The toe is divided into two halves, with a stitch marker at the begininng or end of each half.

52 divided by 2 = 26 - 2 for stitches with stitch markers = 24.

24 divided by 2 = 12 this will be the number of stitches you will work between the markers for the set-up round. From then on, decrease as normal.

AFTERTHOUGHT HEEL

This is the easiest sock construction to adjust, whether you are working toe up or cuff down. As with the heel flap and gusset socks, always add or take away in multiples of 4 stitches.

For this example let's use the Basic sock, cuff down, afterthought heel. For the largest size, we start with 48 stitches, and as before, we would like to increase by 4 stitches. We will work 52 stitches of chainless foundation, then move on to the leg. The leg part has increases placed every few rounds to create ample space for the instep In the pattern, we increase to 54, so with our 4 additional stitches, that will be 58.

When you are ready to separate for the heel, divide the total stitch number by 2:

58 divided by 2 = 29 sts

This will be the stitch number for the heel opening. Make 29 chainless foundation stitches, skip 29 stitches on the socks and continue onto the foot part of the sock. While working on this part you will decrease to bring the stitch count back to the original number.

When you are ready to shape the toes, position a stitch marker to denote the beginning of the round (as in the pattern). The toe is divided into two halves, with stitch markers at the beginning or end of each half.

58 divided by 2 = 29 - 2 for stitches with stitch markers = 27

This is an odd number and does not give us even halves; however, this is adjustable. If we decrease by 2, it will give us 56 sts, which when divided by 2, gives us 28. You can [sc2togBLO] twice on the last round before setting up for the toes. Place this decrease on the sole of the sock.

Now we have 56 divided by 2 = 28 - 2 for stitch markers = 26. 26 divided by 2 = 13

This will be the number of stitches you will work between the markers for the set-up round. From then on decrease as normal.

For the heel, work the same number of stitches as on the chainless foundation and skipped stitches, you can however increase the number to fill up any gaps. Decrease as normal.

Cable Socks

Crochet cables create a very interesting fabric. The cables are made with front post treble crochets, this results in thicker fabric where the cables are. They can also tighten the item, especially on areas where the twists are placed; however, the heel construction in this sock should ensure ample space around the heel and top of foot.

MATERIALS

West Yorkshire Spinners Signature 4ply (75% wool, 25% nylon), 4ply, 400m (437½yd) in a 100g (3½oz) ball, in the following shades:

- Amber (1004) x 1 ball

3mm (US C/2 or D/3) crochet hook (or size required to match tension [gauge])

3 x different colour lockable stitch markers (I will be using green, blue and yellow markers)

TENSION (GAUGE)

After steam blocking: 12 sts and 10 rounds measure 5 x 5cm (2 x 2in) over esc worked in the round using a 3mm (US C/2 or D/3) hook.

15 sts and 9 rounds measure 5 x 5cm (2 x 2in) over cable pattern, worked in the round using a 3mm (US C/2 or D/3) hook.

When you are making your tension swatch make sure it is done in the round as tension can differ between working in rows and rounds.

FINISHED SIZE

Please note that measurements are after steam blocking and that the crochet fabric might stretch more lengthwise and widthwise with wet blocking. Esc stitches have a great stretch to them.

Leg (measured from top of heel to top of cuff) 10cm (4in) in length.

SOCK SIZE	S	M	L
Shoe size UK (US)	3–4 (5–6)	5–6 (7–8)	7–8 (9–10)
Foot circumference (approximate)	16.5cm (6½in)	17cm (6¾in)	20cm (8in)
Foot length (approximate)	19.5cm (7¾in)	22cm (8¾in)	25cm (10in)

Pattern Note

It is important to make the centre single crochets in this pattern as loose as possible. When creating them, pull them to the height of the current row, as you would when working a spike stitch.

Special Stitches

Centre single crochet (csc): *insert hook through the centre of the indicated stitch (between the 'V' shape rather than through the top 2 loops), yo, pull up a loop, yo, draw through both loops on hook.*

Centre single crochet 2b (csc2b): *work csc into csc 2 rows below; insert the hook between the legs of csc two rows below.*

Front post double crochet (FPdc): *yo, insert hook around the post of next st from front to back to front again, yo, pull up a loop, [yo, pull through 2 loops on hook] twice.*

Cable 6 front (c6F): *skip next 3 sts, 3FPdc, working in front of the sts just made, 3FPdc in skipped sts.*

SOCKS (MAKE 2)

CUFF

Using a 3mm (US C/2 or D/3) hook ch9 (9) (9).

Row 1: 1sc in 2nd ch from hook, 1sc in every ch to end, turn. 8 (8) (8) sts

Row 2: ch1 (does not count as a st here and throughout), 1scBLO in every st to end, turn.

Rep row 2 a further 44 (48) (52) times, ending with WS facing for next row.

SEAM CUFF

Hold first and last rows together and, working in BLO of sts of both rows, ch1, sl st across to join. Do not fasten off.

LEG

Rotate piece to work in row-ends of cuff.

Working in row-ends, work 49 (53) (57) hdc evenly spaced around top edge of cuff. Do not join.

Place yellow marker in first st for beginning of round and move marker up as you work.

Continue to work in a continuous spiral.

CABLE PATTERN

Round 1: 25 (27) (29) esc, 2 (3) (4) csc, [c6F, 1csc] 3 times, 1 (2) (3) csc.

Rounds 2 to 4: 25 (27) (29) esc, 2 (3) (4) csc, [6FPdc, 1csc] 3 times, 1 (2) (3) csc.

Rounds 1 to 4 form the cable pattern.

Rep cable pattern 3 more times, then work rounds 1 and 2 once more.

HEEL FLAP

The heel is worked back and forth in rows using sc and csc over half the sock, leaving the rem (top of the foot) sts unworked.

Row 1 (RS): [1sc, 1csc] 12 (13) (14) times, 1sc, leave rem sts unworked, turn. 25 (27) (29) sts

Row 2 (WS) and every WS Row: ch1, 1sc in every st to end, turn.

Row 3: [1sc, 1csc2b] 12 (13) (14) times, 1sc, turn.

Row 5: [1sc, 1csc2b] 12 (13) (14) times, 1sc, turn.

Row 6: As Row 2.

Rep Rows 5 and 6 a further 7 (8) (9) times. Total of 20 (22) (24) rows worked for the heel flap.

TURN HEEL

Row 1 (RS): ch1, 13 (14) (15) sc, 1sc2tog, 1sc in next st, leave rem sts unworked, turn. 15 (16) (17) sts

Row 2: ch1, 3sc, 1sc2tog, 1sc, turn. 5 (5) (5) sts

Row 3: ch1, 1sc in every st to 1 st from end of row, 1sc2tog working the first half of the st in the next st and the second half into the next st 2 rows below, 1sc, turn. 6 (6) (6) sts

Rep Row 3 a further 7 (9) (9) times.

SIZE S AND L ONLY

Next row: ch1, 1sc in every st to 1 st from end of row, 1sc2tog working the first half of the st in the next st and the second half into the next st 2 rows below, turn.

Rep last row once more. 13 (-) (15) sts

All those unworked stitches have been used up and you have turned your heel. 13 (15) (15) sts

ALL SIZES: GUSSET

Round 1 (RS): ch1, 13 (15) (15) sc across heel sts, 11 (12) (13) sc evenly along edge of heel flap (working 1 st in every other row approx.), place blue marker in last st worked, 2 (3) (4) csc, [6FPdc, 1csc] 3 times, 1 (2) (3) csc, 11 (12) (13) sc evenly along edge of heel flap, place green marker in first sc worked. 59 (65) (69) sts

You are now at the end of the round.

Start working in a continuous spiral, placing yellow marker in first st of Round 2 to denote the beg of round.

Move markers up as you work.

Round 2: 1esc in every st to 2 sts before blue marker, 1esc2tog, 1esc in marked st, 2 (3) (4) csc, [6FPdc, 1csc] 3 times, 1 (2) (3) csc, 1esc in marked st, 1esc2tog, 1sc in every st to end. 57 (63) (67) sts

Round 3: 1esc in every st to blue marker, 1esc in marked st, 2 (3) (4) csc, [C6F, 1csc] 3 times, 1 (2) (3) csc, 1esc in marked st, 1esc in every st to end.

Round 4: As Round 2. 55 (61) (65) sts

Round 5: 1esc in every st to blue marker, 1esc in marked st, 2 (3) (4) csc, [6FPdc, 1csc] 3 times, 1 (2) (3) csc, 1esc in st with green marker, 1esc in every st to end.

Round 6: As Round 2. 53 (59) (63) sts

Rep Rounds 3 to 6 once more. 49 (55) (59) sts

SIZES M AND L ONLY

Rep Rounds 3 and 4 once more. (53) (57) sts

ALL SIZES

Keep all markers in place.

For S size: starting with Round 1 of cable pattern, rep Rounds 1 to 4 a further 4 times, then rep Rounds 1 and 2 once more, ending last repeat at green marker. The foot should measure 15.5cm (6in) from the back of the heel.

For M and L sizes: starting with Round 3 of cable pattern, repeat Round 4, then work Rounds 1 to 4 of cable pattern – (4) (5) times, then rep Rounds 1 and 2 once more, ending last rep at green marker. The foot should measure – (17) (18.5)cm/(6¾) (7¼)in from the back of the heel.

Next round: Place green marker in last csc st made, 1esc2tog, 1esc in every st to 1 st before blue marker, remove marker, 1esc2tog, 1csc in next st, place blue marker in st just made, 1sc in every st to green marker, 1csc in marked st, this is now the beg of round. 47 (51) (55) sts

The yellow marker can now be removed, keeping the blue and green markers in place

TOE

Round 1: 1sc2tog, 1sc in every st to 2 sts before blue marker, 1sc2tog, 1csc in marked st, 1sc2tog, 1sc in every st to 2 sts before green marker, 1sc2tog, 1csc in marked st. 43 (47) (51) sts

Round 2: 1sc in every st to blue marker, 1csc in marked st, 1sc in every st to green marker, 1csc in marked st.

Rep Rounds 1 and 2 a further 4 (5) (6) times.

Rep Round 1 once more. 23 (23) (23) sts

Fasten off leaving a yarn tail approximately 15cm (6in) in length. Thread tail onto tapestry needle and, making sure toe is correctly aligned with heel, sew toe opening closed. Weave in the yarn end.

FINISHING

Weave in ends and block as preferred (see Finishing and Caring for Socks).

CHART

The chart shows only the cable section.

The chart is read from right to left on every round.

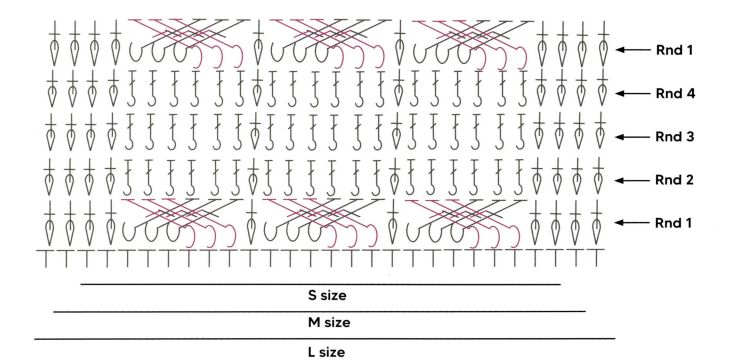

← Rnd 1

← Rnd 4

← Rnd 3

← Rnd 2

← Rnd 1

S size

M size

L size

KEY

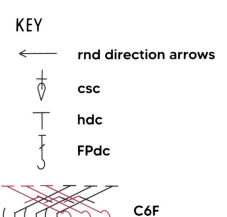

← rnd direction arrows

csc

hdc

FPdc

C6F

Spike Stitch Socks

These charming socks are not only fun to wear, but also a joy to make. Choose bold colours for the backround and a gentler tone for the spike stitches, cuff, heel and toe. Or vice versa! They are a great design for experimenting with colour.

MATERIALS

John Arbon Textiles Exmoor Socks (60% Exmoor Blueface, 20% Corriedale, 10% Zwartbles, 10% nylon) 4ply, 200m (218¾yd) in 50g (1¾oz) skein (hank), in the following shade:

- A – Plashes x (1) (1) (2) skeins (hanks)

Felt Fusion for John Arbon (60% Exmoor Blueface, 20% Corriedale, 10% Zwartbles, 10% nylon) 4ply, 400m (437½yd) in a 100g (3½oz) skein (hank), in the following shade:

- B – Down Devon Way x 1 (1) (1) skein (hank)

3mm (US C/2 or D/3) crochet hook (or size required to match tension [gauge])

3 x different colour lockable stitch markers (I will be using green, blue and yellow)

Note that Down Devon Way is a special edition of John Arbon yarn, but there are many beautiful hand-dyed yarns from indie dyers that can be used as an alternative.

TENSION (GAUGE)

After steam blocking: 12 sts and 13 rounds measure 5 x 5cm (2 x 2in) over scBLO, worked in the round using a 3mm (US C/2 or D/3) hook. When you are making your tension swatch make sure it is done in the round as tension can differ between working in rows and rounds.

FINISHED SIZE

Please note that measurements are after steam blocking and that the crochet fabric might stretch more lengthwise and widthwise with wet blocking.

Leg – measured from top of heel to top of cuff – 17cm (6¾in) in length.

SOCK SIZE	S	M	L
Shoe size UK (US)	3-4 (5-6)	5-6 (7-8)	7-8 (9-10)
Foot circumference (approximate)	18.5cm (7¼in)	20cm (8in)	21.5cm (8½in)
Foot length (approximate)	21cm (8¼in)	23cm (9in)	25cm (10in)

Please note that these measurements were taken before blocking and that the crochet fabric will stretch lengthwise and widthwise.

Pattern Note

The socks have lots of positive ease, if you would like tighter socks make the smaller size. The cuff down construction with heel flap offers ample space around the heel and top of foot.

Special Stitch

Spike single crochet (ssc): Insert hook in st in round(s) below (as indicated), yo, pull loop through and up to height of current round, yo, pull through both loops on hook.

RIGHT SOCK

CUFF

Using yarn A, ch13 (13) (13).

Row 1 (RS): 1sc in 2nd ch from hook, 1sc in every ch, turn 12. (12) (12) sts

Row 2: ch1 (does not count as a st here and throughout), 1scBLO in every st, turn.

Rep Row 2 a further 40 (44) (48) times, ending with WS facing for the next row.

SEAM CUFF

Hold first and last rows together and, working in BLO of sts of both rows, ch 1, sl st across to join. Do not fasten off.

LEG

Rotate piece to work in row-ends of cuff.

Next round: Working in row-ends, ch1, 44 (48) (52) sc evenly spaced around top edge of cuff.

Do not join.

Place yellow marker in first st for beginning of round and move marker up as you work.

Continue to work in a continuous spiral.

Pattern note: You will work using yarn B for 4 rounds and yarn A for 1 round. Do not fasten off colours, carry them up with you as you work, catching A at the back on every round.

Join yarn B.

Rounds 1 to 4: 1scBLO in every st to end.

Change to yarn A.

Round 5: * 1scBLO, 1 spike-sc in next st 3 rounds below; rep from * to end. 22 (24) (26) spikes made

Rounds 1 to 5 form the pattern.

Rep pattern 4 more times. **

Next 2 rounds: Using yarn B, 1scBLO in every st to end.

Fasten off yarn B.

HEEL FLAP

Work heel flap and heel turn in yarn A.

For the heel flap you will work back and forth in rows using sc and FPdc.

Row 1 (RS): ch1, 21 (23) (25) sc, leave rem sts unworked, turn. 21 (23) (25) sts

Row 2: ch1, 1sc in every st to end, turn.

Row 3: ch1, * 1sc in next st, 1FPdc around post of next st 3 rows below; rep from * to last st, 1sc, turn.

Row 4: ch1, 1sc in every st to end of row, turn.

Rep Rows 3 and 4 a further 8 (9) (10) times, ending with RS facing for next row.

Total of 20 (22) (24) rows worked on the heel.

TURN HEEL

Row 1: ch1, 10 (11) (12) sc, 1sc2tog, 1sc, leave rem sts unworked, turn. 12 (13) (14) sts

Row 2: ch1, 1sc, 1sc2tog, 1sc, turn. 3 (3) (3) sts

Row 3: ch1, 1sc in every st to 1 st from end of row, 1sc2tog working the first half of the st in the next st and the second half in the next st 2 rows below, 1sc, turn. 4 (4) (4) sts

Rep Row 3 a further 7 (7) (9) times. 11 (11) (13) sts

SIZE M ONLY

Next row: ch1, 1sc in every st to 1 st from end of row, 1sc2tog working the first half of the st in the next st and the second half in the next st 2 rows below, turn.

Rep last row once more. - (11) (-) sts

All those unworked stitches have been used up and you have turned your heel. 11 (11) (13) sts

ALL SIZES: GUSSET

Join yarn B.

Round 1 (RS): ch1, 10 (11) (13) sc across heel sts, 11 (12) (13) sc evenly along edge of heel flap, (working 1 st every other row approx.), place blue marker in last st worked, 23 (25) (27) scBLO across sts of foot, 11 (12) (13) sc evenly along edge of heel flap, place green marker in first st worked. 56 (60) (66) sts

You are at the end of the round.

Start working in a continuous spiral, placing yellow marker in first st of Round 2 to denote the beg of round.

You will now work in pattern across the sts for the top of foot, and in scBLO on the sts for the sole.

For the first 2 rounds you will work a csc in sts marked with blue and green markers, then for the remaining rounds you will work a spike single crochet in these sts.

Move all markers up as you work.

Round 2: 1scBLO in every st to 2 sts before blue marker, 1sc2togBLO, 1csc in marked st, 1scBLO in every st to green marker, 1csc in marked st, 1sc2togBLO, 1scBLO in every st to end. 54 (58) (64) sts

Change to yarn A.

Round 3: 1scBLO in every st to blue marker, 1csc in marked st, [1scBLO, 1spike-sc in next st 3 rnds below] 11 (12) (13) times, 1scBLO, 1csc in marked st, 1scBLO in every st to end.

Change to yarn B.

Round 4: 1scBLO in every st to 2 sts before blue marker, 1sc2togBLO, 1spike-sc in marked st, inserting hook in between the two legs of csc 2 rnds below, 1scBLO in every st to next marker, 1spike-sc in marked st, inserting hook in between the two legs of csc 2 rnds below, 1sc2togBLO, 1scBLO in every st to end. 52 (56) (62) sts

Round 5: 1scBLO in every st to blue marker, 1spike-sc in marked st, inserting hook in between the two legs of csc 2 rnds below,1scBLO in every st to next marker, 1spike-sc in marked st, inserting hook in between the two legs of csc 2 rnds below, 1scBLO in every st to end.

Round 6: 1scBLO in every st to 2 sts before blue marker, 1sc2togBLO, 1spike-sc in marked st, inserting hook in between the two legs of spike-sc 2 rows below, 1scBLO in every st to next marker, 1spike-sc in marked st, inserting hook in between the two legs of spike-sc 2 rows below, 1sc2tog BLO, 1scBLO in every st to end. 50 (54) (60) sts

Round 7: 1scBLO in every st to blue marker, 1spike-sc in marked st, inserting hook in between the two legs of spike-sc 2 rnds below, 1scBLO in every st to next marker, 1spike-sc in st with maker, inserting hook in between the two legs of spike-sc 2 rnds below, 1scBLO in every st to end.

Change to yarn A.

Round 8: 1scBLO in every st to 2 sts before blue marker, 1sc2togBLO, 1 spike-sc in marked st, inserting hook in between the two legs of spike-sc 2 rnds below, [1scBLO, 1spike-sc in next st 3 rnds below] 11 (12) (13) times, 1scBLO, 1spike-sc in marked st, inserting hook in between the two legs of spike-sc 2 rnds below, 1sc2togBLO, 1scBLO in every st to end. 48 (52) (58) sts

Change to yarn B.

Round 9: 1scBLO in every st to blue marker, 1 spike-sc in marked st inserting hook in between the two legs of spike-sc 2 rnds below,1scBLO in every st to next marker, 1spike-sc in marked st, inserting hook in between the two legs of spike-sc 2 rnds below, 1scBLO in every st to end.

Round 10: 1scBLO in every st to 2 sts before blue marker, 1sc2tog BLO, 1 spike-sc in marked st inserting hook in between the two legs of spike-sc 2 rows below, 1scBLO in every st to next marker, 1 spike-sc in marked st inserting hook in between the two legs of spike-sc 2 rows below, 1sc2tog BLO, 1scBLO in every st to end. 46 (50) (56) sts

Rep Rounds 9 and 10 once more. 44 (48) (54) sts

SIZE L ONLY

Change to yarn A

Round 13: 1scBLO in every st to st with blue marker, 1spike-sc in marked st, inserting hook in between the two legs of spike-sc 2 rnds below, [1scBLO, 1spike-sc in next st 3 rnds below] 13 times, 1scBLO, 1spike-sc in marked st, inserting hook in between the two legs of spike-sc 2 rnds below, 1scBLO in every st to end.

Change to yarn B.

Round 14: 1scBLO in every st to 2 sts before blue marker, 1sc2tog BLO, 1spike-sc in marked st inserting hook in between the two legs of spike-sc 2 rows below, 1scBLO in every st to next marker, 1spike-sc in marked st inserting hook in between the two legs of spike-sc 2 rows below, 1sc2togBLO, 1scBLO in every st to end. - (-) (52) sts

Foot: Sizes S and M only

Change to yarn A.

Round 13: 1scBLO in every st to st with blue marker, 1spike-sc in marked st inserting hook in between the two legs of spike-sc 2 rnds below, [1scBLO, 1spike-sc in next st 3 rnds below] 11 (12) (-) times, 1scBLO, 1spike-sc in st with marker, inserting hook in between the two legs of spike-sc 2 rnds below, 1scBLO in every st to end. 44 (48) (-) sts

Change to yarn B.

Round 14: 1scBLO in every st to st with blue marker, 1spike-sc in marked st, inserting hook in between the two legs of spike-sc 2 rows below, 1scBLO in every st to next marker, 1 spike-sc in marked st, inserting hook in between the two legs of spike-sc 2 rows below, 1scBLO in every st to end.

ALL SIZES

Using yarn B.

Rounds 15 to 17: 1scBLO in every st to st with blue marker, 1spike-sc in marked st, inserting hook in between the two legs of spike-sc 2 rows below, 1scBLO in every st to next marker, 1spike-sc in marked st, inserting hook in between the two legs of spike-sc 2 rows below, 1scBLO in every st to end.

Change to yarn A.

Round 18: 1scBLO in every st to st with blue marker, 1spike-sc in marked st, inserting hook in between the two legs of spike-sc 2 rnds below, [1scBLO, 1spike-sc in next st 3 rnds below] 11 (12) (13) times, 1scBLO, 1spike-sc in marked st inserting hook in between the two legs of spike-sc 2 rnds below, 1scBLO in every st to end.

Change to yarn B.

Round 19: 1scBLO in every st to st with blue marker, 1spike-sc in marked st, inserting hook in between the two legs of spike-sc 2 rows below, 1scBLO in every st to next marker, 1spike-sc in marked st, inserting hook in between the two legs of spike-sc 2 rows below, 1scBLO in every st to end.

Rep Rounds 15 to 19 a further 3 (4) (5) more times, changing colour as set.

Next round: As round 19.

TOE

Fasten off yarn B and continue with yarn A.

Work in scBLO to blue marker, this is now the beg of round. The yellow marker can now be removed.

Round 1: 1scBLO in stitch with blue marker, 1sc2tog BLO, 19 (21) (23) scBLO, 1sc2tog BLO, 1scBLO in next st with green maker, 1scBLO to end. 42 (46) (50) sts

You will now work in sc.

Round 2: 1sc in every st to end, moving markers up as you work.

Round 3: 1sc in stitch with blue marker, 1sc2tog, 1sc in every st to 2 sts before green marker, 1sc2tog, 1sc in marked st, 1sc2tog, 1sc in every st to 2 sts before blue marker, 1sc2tog. 38 (42) (46) sts

Rep Rounds 2 and 3 a further 4 (5) (6) times. 22 (22) (22) sts

Fasten off leaving a yarn tail of approximately 15cm (6in). Thread yarn tail onto a tapestry needle and, making sure toe is correctly aligned with heel, sew toe opening closed. Weave in the yarn end.

FINISHING

Weave in ends and block as preferred (see Finishing and Caring for Socks).

LEFT SOCK

Work as for Right sock until **

Next round: Using yarn B, 1scBLO in every st to end.

HEEL FLAP

Row 1 (RS): Using yarn B, 23 (25) (27) scBLO, change to yarn A and fasten off B. Using yarn A, 21 (23) (25) sc, turn.

Starting from Row 2 of heel flap, work remainder of Left sock as for Right sock.

Simple Overlay Crochet Socks

This sock project is an ideal way to start your adventure with the overlay mosaic technique. The pattern consists of single crochet worked in the back and front loops and double crochet worked into the front loop two rounds down.

MATERIALS

Hjertegarn Longcolors (75% superwash wool, 25% nylon), 4ply, 400m (437½yd) in a 100g (3½oz) ball, in the following shade:

- A – Orchard (600) x 1 ball

Lang Yarns Jawoll Silk Superwash (55% wool, 25% nylon, 20% silk), 4ply, 200m (218¾yd) in 50g (1¾oz) ball, in the following shade:

- B – Cream (194) x 1 ball

3mm (US C/2 or D/3) crochet hook (or size required to match tension [gauge])

2 x different colour lockable stitch markers (I'll be using green and blue markers)

TENSION (GAUGE)

After steam blocking: 13 sts and 11 rounds measure 5 x 5cm (2 x 2in) over overlay mosaic pattern, worked in the round using a 3mm (US C/2 or D/3) hook.

When you are making your tension swatch make sure it is done in the round as tension can differ between working in rows and rounds.

FINISHED SIZE

Please note that measurements are after steam blocking and that the crochet fabric might stretch more lengthwise and widthwise with wet blocking.

Leg – measured from top of heel to top of cuff – 12cm (4¾in) in length.

SOCK SIZE	S	M	L
Shoe size UK (US)	3-4 (5-6)	5-6 (7-8)	7-8 (9-10)
Foot circumference (approximate)	15cm (6in)	17.5cm (7in)	19cm (7½in)
Foot length (approximate)	21cm (8¼in)	23cm (9in)	25cm (10in)

Pattern Note

These socks are worked using overlay mosaic technique. If you have never crocheted using this technique, this is the perfect place to start. The easily memorized pattern repeat works up very quickly.

Use high contrast colours to make the pattern stand out. Do not break off yarn after every round, instead carry it up the work with you.

Special Stitch

Front loop double crochet 2 down (FLdc2d): *Working in front of sts from previous row, work a double crochet in FLO of st 2 rows below.*

RIGHT SOCK

CUFF

Using a 3mm (US C/2 or D/3) hook and yarn A, 42 (46) (50) chainless foundation sc, join with sl st to form a loop.

Place green marker in first st to denote the beg of round. Move marker up as you work.

Round 1 (RS): ch1 (does not count as a st here and throughout), 1hdc in every st to end.

Round 2: ch1, * 1FPdc around next st, 1BPdc around next st, rep from * to end, sl st to first st.

Rep last round twice more.

LEG

Round 1: Work 46 (50) (54) scBLO evenly around, do not join. 46 (50) (54) sts

Continue to work in a continuous spiral using the overlay mosaic technique.

Change to yarn B.

Round 2: 1scBLO in every st to end.

Change to yarn A.

Round 3: *1scBLO, 1FLdc2d, rep from * to end.

Change to yarn B.

Round 4: As round 2.

Change to yarn A.

Round 5: 1scBLO in every st to end.

Rounds 2 to 5 set the pattern, rep pattern twice more changing colour as set, then rep Rounds 2 and 3 once more.

Next round: [2scBLO in next st, 22 (24) (26) scBLO] twice. 48 (52) (56) sts

Starting with Round 5, work in pattern, changing colour as set, for 7 more rounds, ending with Round 3. **

SEPARATING FOR HEEL

Change to yarn B.

Next round: Chainless foundation 24 (26) (28) sc, skip next 24 (26) (28) sts, 1scBLO in every st to end.

Change to yarn A.

Starting with Round 5 of pattern, work pattern changing colour as set for 11 rounds, ending with Round 3 of pattern.

Change to yarn B.

Next round: [1sc2togBLO, 22 (24) (26) scBLO] twice. 46 (50) (54) sts

Change to yarn A.

Starting with Round 5 of pattern, work in pattern changing colour as set for 3 rounds, ending with Round 3 of pattern.

Change to yarn B.

Next round: [1sc2togBLO, 21 (23) (25) scBLO] twice. 44 (48) (52) sts

Change to yarn A.

Starting with Round 5 of pattern, work in pattern changing colour as set for 3 rounds, ending with Round 3 of pattern.

Change to yarn B.

Next round: [1sc2togBLO, 20 (22) (24) scBLO] twice. 42 (46) (50) sts

Change to yarn A.

Starting with Round 5 of pattern, work in pattern changing colour as set until work measures 11 (13) (15)cm/4¼ (5) (6)in from heel opening, ending with Round 4 of pattern.

TOE

Fasten off yarn B, continue with yarn A.

Round 1: 1scBLO in first st (keep green marker in this st), 1sc2tog BLO, 16 (18) (20) scBLO, 1sc2togBLO, 1scBLO in next st, place blue marker in st just made, 1sc2togBLO, 1scBLO in every st to 2 sts before green marker, sc2tog. 38 (42) (46) sts

Move markers up as you work.

Round 2: 1sc in st with green marker, 1sc in every st around to green marker.

Round 3: 1sc in st with green marker, 1sc2tog, 1sc in every st to 2 sts before blue marker, 1sc2tog, 1sc in marked st, 1sc2tog, 1sc in every st to 2 sts before green marker, 1sc2tog. 34 (38) (42) sts

Rep Rounds 2 and 3 a further 3 (4) (5) times. 22 (22) (22) sts

Fasten off leaving a tail of approximately 15cm (6in). Using a tapestry needle and tail, sew toe opening closed. Weave in the yarn end.

AFTERTHOUGHT HEEL

Heel is worked in a continuous spiral.

With RS facing, join yarn B at the bottom right corner of heel opening, working along the sole, work 24 (26) (28) sc, 1sc in gap in between the stitches at corner, place blue marker in last st made. Working along the other side of the opening (the leg part), work 24 (26) (28) sc, 1sc in gap in between the stitches at corner, place green marker in last st made. 50 (54) (58) sts

Move markers up as you work.

Round 1: 1sc2tog, 1sc in every st to 2 sts before blue marker, 1sc2tog, 1sc in marked st, 1sc2tog, 1sc in every st to 2 sts before green marker, 1sc2tog, 1sc in marked st. 46 (50) (54) sts

Round 2: 1sc in every st to end.

Rep Rounds 1 and 2 a further 6 (6) (6) more times, then work Round 1 once more. 22 (26) (30) sts

Fasten off leaving a tail of approximately 15cm (6in). Using a tapestry needle and tail, sew the heel opening closed. Weave in the yarn end.

LEFT SOCK

Work as for Right sock to **.

Change to yarn B.

Next round: 24 (26) (28) scBLO, chainless foundation 24 (26) (28) sc changing to yarn A on last sc, skip next 24 (26) (28) sts.

Change to yarn A by working the last chainless foundation st to two loops on hook, finish the st with A.

Starting with Round 5 of pattern, work pattern changing colour as set for 11 rounds, ending with Round 3 of pattern.

Work remainder of Left sock as for Right sock.

> **Tip**
>
> This pattern will work wonderfully in many combinations of colours - try experimenting with speckly yarn and solid yarn or two solids.

CHART

The chart is a visiual representation of the overlay mosaic crochet.

The chart is read from right to left on every round.

The column marked with 0 is a colour indicator column. Do not include this column in the pattern repeat.

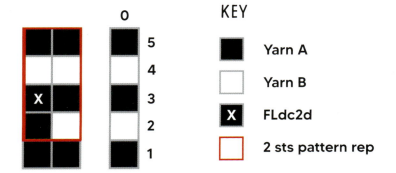

KEY

- ■ Yarn A
- □ Yarn B
- ☒ FLdc2d
- ☐ 2 sts pattern rep

One Colour Rib Socks

The ribbing on these socks is made using front-post half double and single crochet stitches. It creates a beautiful effect running down the sock. It also results in a fabric with plenty of stretch and great fit. This stitch is ideal for all types of yarns, from variegated and gradient to solid colour.

MATERIALS

Rowan Sock (75% wool, 25% polyamide), 4ply, 400m (437½yd) in a 100g (3½oz) ball, in the following shade:

• Jewel (001) x 1 ball

3mm (US C/2 or D/3) crochet hook (or size required to match tension [gauge])

2 x different colour lockable stitch markers (I'll be using green and blue markers)

TENSION (GAUGE)

After steam blocking: 13 sts and 10 rnds measure 5 x 5cm (2 x 2in) over pattern (sc and FPhdc) worked in the round using a 3mm (US C/2 or D/3) hook.

When you are making your tension swatch make sure it is done in the round as tension can differ between working in rows and rounds.

FINISHED SIZE

Please note that measurements are after steam blocking and that the crochet fabric might stretch more lengthwise and widthwise with wet blocking. Esc stitches have a great stretch to them.

Leg – measured from top of heel to top of cuff – 17cm (6¾in) in length.

SOCK SIZE	S	M	L
Shoe size UK (US)	3-4 (5-6)	5-6 (7-8)	7-8 (9-10)
Foot circumference (approximate)	17cm (6¾in)	18.5cm (7¼in)	20cm (8in)
Foot length (approximate)	21cm (8¼in)	23cm (9in)	25cm (10in)

Pattern Note

If you are working with self-striping yarn, you need to begin each sock with the same colour sequence so that your socks will match.

RIGHT SOCK

CUFF

Using a 3mm (US C/2 or D/3) hook, ch11 (11) (11).

Row 1: 1sc in 2nd ch from hook, 1sc in every ch, turn. 10 (10) (10) sts

Row 2: ch1 (does not count as a st here and throughout), 1scBLO in every st, turn.

Rep row 2 a further 44 (48) (52) times, ending with WS facing for the next row. (46, 50, 54 rows in total)

SEAM CUFF

Hold first and last rows together and, working in BLO of sts of both rows, ch1, sl st across to join. Do not fasten off.

LEG

Rotate piece to work in row-ends of cuff.

Next round: ch1, 48 (52) (56) esc evenly spaced around top edge of cuff, sl st in first st to join.

Round 1: ch1 (does not count as a st here and throughout), 1sc in same st as sl st, 1FPhdc around next st, * 1sc, 1FPhdc around next st; rep from * to end, sl st in first sc to join.

Round 2: ch1, 1sc in same st as sl st, 1FPhdc around next FPhdc, * 1sc, 1FPhdc around next FPhdc; rep from * to end, sl st in first sc to join.

Rounds 3 to 15: As Round 2.

Round 16: ch1, 1sc3tog, 1FPhdc around next FPhdc, * 1sc, 1FPhdc around of next FPhdc; rep from * to end, sl st in first sc to join. 46 (50) (54) sts

Rounds 17 to 26: Rep Round 2. **

SEPARATING FOR HEEL

Round 27: 23 (25) (27) chainless foundation sc, skip next 23 (25) (27) sts, 1FPhdc around next FPhdc, * 1sc, 1FPhdc around next FPhdc; rep from * to end, sl st in first sc of chainless foundation to join.

Round 28: ch1, 1sc in same st as sl st, 1sc in every st of chainless foundation, 1FPhdc around next st, * 1sc, 1FPhdc around of next FPhdc; rep from * to end, sl st in first sc to join.

FOOT

Round 29: ch1, 1scBLO in same st as sl st, 22 (24) (26) scBLO, 1FPhdc around next st, * 1sc, 1FPhdc around next FPhdc; rep from * to end, sl st in first sc to join.

Rep Round 29 twice more.

Round 32: ch1, 1sc2tog BLO, 19 (21) (23) scBLO, 1sc2tog BLO, 1FPhdc around next FPhdc, * 1sc, 1FPhdc around next FPhdc; rep from * to end, sl st in first sc to join. 44 (48) (52) sts

Round 33: ch1, 1scBLO in same st as sl st, 20 (22) (24) scBLO, 1FPhdc around next st, * 1sc, 1FPhdc around next FPhdc; rep from * to end, sl st in first sc to join.

Rep Round 33 until foot measures 11 (13) (15)cm/4¼ (5) (6)in from chainless foundation (of separating for heel).

TOES

The toe is worked in a continuous spiral.

Set-up round: ch1, 1sc in same st as sl st, 20 (22) (24) sc, 1sc in next st, place green marker st just made, 21 (23) (25) sc, 1sc in next st, place blue marker in st just made, this is now the beg of rnd.

Round 1: 1sc2tog, 1sc in every st to 2 sts before green marker, 1sc2tog, 1sc in marked st, 1sc2tog, 1sc in every st to 2 sts before blue marker, 1sc2tog, 1sc in marked st. 40 (44) (48) sts

Round 2: 1sc in every st to end, moving markers up as you work.

Rep Rounds 1 and 2 a further 3 (4) (5) times.

Rep Round 1 once more. 24 (24) (24) sts

Fasten off leaving a tail of approximately 15cm (6in). Thread yarn tail onto a tapestry needle and sew toe opening closed. Weave in the yarn end.

AFTERTHOUGHT HEEL

The heel is worked in a continuous spiral.

With RS facing, join yarn with 1sc at the bottom right corner of heel opening. Working along the sole, work 23 (25) (27) sc, place green marker in last st made. Working along the other side of opening (the leg part), work 23 (25) (27) sc, place blue marker in last st made. 46 (50) (54) sts

Round 1: 1sc2tog, 1sc in every st to 2 sts before green marker, 1sc2tog, 1sc in marked st, 1sc2tog, 1sc in every st to 2 sts before blue marker, 1sc2tog, 1sc in marked st. 42 (46) (50) sts

Round 2: 1sc in every st to end, moving markers up as you work.

Rep Rounds 1 and 2 a further 4 (4) (4) times.

Rep Round 1 once more. 22 (26) (30) sts

Fasten off leaving a tail of approximately 15cm (6in). Thread yarn tail onto a tapestry needle and sew heel closed. Weave in the yarn end.

LEFT SOCK

Work as for Right foot to **.

SEPARATING FOR HEEL

Round 27: ch1, 1sc in same st as sl st, 1FPhdc around next FPhdc, [1sc, 1FPhdc around next FPhdc] 11 (12) (13) times, 23 (25) (27) chainless foundation sc, skip next 23 (25) (27) sts (including first sc made in this round), sl st in first FPhdc to join, this is now the beg of round. 46 (50) (54) sts

Round 28: ch1, 1FPhdc around the first FPhdc, [1sc, 1FPhdc around next FPhdc] 11 (12) (13) times, 1sc in every st of chainless foundation, sl st in first st to join.

Round 29: ch1, 1FPhdc around the first FPhdc, [1sc, 1FPhdc around next FPhdc] 11 (12) (13) times, 1scBLO in every st end, sl st to first st.

Rep Round 29 twice more.

Round 32: ch1, 1FPhdc around the first FPhdc, [1sc, 1FPhdc around next FPhdc] 11 (12) (13) times, 1sc2tog BLO, 19 (21) (23) scBLO, 1sc2tog BLO, sl st in first st to join. 44 (48) (52) sts

Rep Round 29 until foot measures 11 (13) (15)cm/4.5 (5) (6)in from chainless foundation (of separating from heel).

TOES

The toe is worked in a continuous spiral.

Set-up Round: ch1, 1sc in same st as sl st, place blue marker in st just made, 21 (23) (25) sc, 1sc in next st, place green marker in st just made. 21 (23) (25) sts

Move markers up as you work.

Round 1: 1sc in st with blue marker, 1sc2tog, 11sc in every st to 2 sts before green marker, 1sc2tog, 1sc in marked st, 1sc2tog, 1sc in every st to 2 sts before blue marker, 1sc2tog. 40 (44) (48) sts

Round 2: 1sc in every st to end.

Rep Rounds 1 and 2 a further 3 (4) (5) times. 28 (28) (28) sts

Rep Round 1 once more. 24 (24) (24) sts

Fasten off leaving a tail of approximately 15cm (6in). Thread yarn tail onto a tapestry needle and sew toe opening closed. Weave in the yarn end.

Work the afterthought heel as for Right foot.

Crochet Fair Isle Pine Tree Socks

These socks are perfect for cosy, wintry nights, snuggling under a blanket. They only come in one size; however, they can easily be adjusted to fit a range of feet.

MATERIALS

Sandes Garn Sisu Superwash (80% wool, 20% nylon) 3ply, 175m (82yd) in a 50g (1¾oz) ball, in the following shades:

- A – Cream (1002) x 2 balls
- B – Pine Green (8063) x 1 ball

3mm (US C/2 or D/3) crochet hook (or size required to match tension [gauge])

2 x easily removable different coloured markers (I'll be using green and blue markers)

TENSION (GAUGE)

After steam blocking: 12 sts and 9 rounds measure 5 x 5cm (2 x 2in) over esc worked in the round using a 3mm (US C/2 or D/3) hook.

Fair Isle tension

11 sts and 13 rounds measure 5 x 5cm (2 x 2in) over csc using the Fair Isle technique worked in the round using a 3mm (US C/2 or D/3) hook.

When you are making your tension swatch make sure it is done in the round as tension can differ between working in rows and rounds.

FINISHED SIZE

Please note that measurements are after steam blocking and that the crochet fabric might stretch more lengthwise and widthwise with wet blocking. Esc stitches have a great stretch to them.

Leg – measured from top of heel to top of picot edge – 14cm (5½in) in length.

SOCK SIZE	M
Shoe size UK (US)	5-6 (7-8)
Foot circumference (approximate)	20cm (8in)
Foot length (approximate)	22cm (8¾in)

Pattern Notes

The centre single crochet stitch used to create the Fair Isle bands results in a gorgeous colourwork effect, but the fabric has little stretch. Use a 3.5mm (US E/4) hook to achieve a larger fit and work more rows for the foot length as required.

For a smaller size, switch to a 2.5mm (US B/1 or C/2) hook and work fewer rows for the foot.

The colour-work band and toes measure approximately 10cm (4in).

RIGHT SOCK

CUFF

Using 3mm (US C/2 or D/3) hook and yarn B, ch9.

Row 1: 1sc in second ch from hook, 1sc in every ch, turn. 8 sts

Row 2: ch1 (does not count as a st here and throughout), 1scBLO in every st, turn.

Rep row 2 a further 46 times (48 rows worked in total) ending with the WS facing for the next row.

SEAM CUFF

Hold first and last rows together and, working in BLO of sts of both rows, ch1, sl st across to join. Do not fasten off.

LEG

Rotate the piece to work in the row-ends of the cuff.

Next round: Working in row-ends, ch1, 50esc evenly spaced around top edge of cuff, sl st to first st to join.

You will now work from Chart A, using csc and the Fair Isle technique (see Special Crochet Techniques).

Work rounds 1 to 17, repeating the 10-st pattern repeat 5 times around sock.

You will now work only in esc.

Do not remove the marker, keep it in place to denote the beginning of round and move it up as you work.

Fasten off yarn B and continue using yarn A.

Rounds 18 to 22: 1esc in every st to end.

Round 23: [1esc2tog, 23 esc] twice. 48 sts

Rounds 24 to 28: As Round 18. **

SEPARATING FOR HEEL

Round 29: 24 chainless foundation sc, skip next 24 sts, 1esc in every st to end.

Round 30: 24esc across foundation sts, 1esc in every st to end.

CHARTS

Each square represents 1 stitch.

The charts are read from right to left on every round.

Repeat the pattern 5 times.

Work in a continuous spiral, placing a blue stitch marker to denote the beginning of round.

Continue working from chart until all rounds have been completed.

CHART A

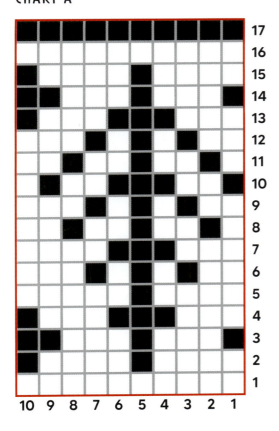

CHART B

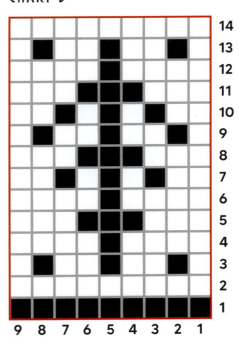

KEY

☐	A
■	B
☐	pattern rep

FOOT

Rounds 31 to 33: As Round 18.

Round 34: [1esc2tog, 22 esc] twice. 46 sts

Rep Round 18 until foot measures 7cm (3in) from chainless foundation of separating for heel. Keep marker in place.

Next round: 1esc2tog, 1esc in every st to end. 45 sts

Join yarn B and work from Chart B using csc and the Fair Isle technique.

Work rounds 1 to 13, repeating the 9-st pattern repeat 5 times around sock.

Round 14: 2csc in first st, 1csc in every st to end. 46 sts

TOE

The toe is worked in sc.

Fasten off yarn A and continue using yarn B.

Round 1: 1sc2tog, 18sc, 1sc2tog, 1sc, place green marker in st just made, 1sc2tog, 1sc in every st to 2 sts before blue marker, 1sc2tog, 1sc in marked st. 42 sts

Round 2: 1sc in every st to end, moving markers up as you work.

Round 3: 1sc2tog, 1sc in every st to 2 sts before green marker, 1sc2tog, 1sc in marked st, 1sc2tog, 1sc in every st to 2 sts before blue marker, 1sc2tog, 1sc in marked st. 38 sts

Rep Rounds 2 and 3 a further 4 times. 22 sts

Fasten off leaving a yarn tail of approximately 15cm (6in). Using a tapestry needle and yarn tail, sew toe opening closed. Weave in the end.

AFTERTHOUGHT HEEL

The heel is worked in sc in a continuous spiral. Note that extra stitches are worked around the heel opening to help prevent any holes forming at the point where you separated for the heel.

With RS facing, join yarn B with 1sc at the bottom right corner of the heel opening. Working along the sole, work 26 sc evenly spaced, place green marker on last st made. Working along the other side of opening (the leg part), 26 sc evenly spaced, place blue marker in last st made. 52 sts

Round 1: 1sc2tog, 1sc in every st to 2 sts before green marker, 1sc2tog, 1sc in marked st, 1sc2tog, 1sc in every st to 2 sts before blue marker, 1sc2tog, 1sc in marked st. 48 sts

Round 2: 1sc in every st to end, moving markers as you work.

Rep Rounds 1 and 2 a further 5 times, ending last rep with Round 1. 28 sts

Fasten off leaving a yarn tail of approximately 15cm (6in). Using a tapestry needle and yarn tail, sew heel opening closed. Weave in the end.

FINISHING

Weave in ends and block as preferred (see Finishing and Caring for Socks).

Tip

The key to success in Fair Isle crochet and center single crochet is maintaining loose tension to help prevent puckering.

LEFT SOCK

Work as for Right Sock until **.

SEPARATING FOR HEEL

Round 29: 24esc, 24 chainless foundation sc, miss next 24 sts.

Round 30: 24esc, 24esc across foundation sts. 48 sts

Work remainder of Left sock as for Right sock.

Lace Socks

Lace socks are perfect for wearing in the Spring. Pair them with your favourite trainers, brogues or jelly shoes. They are also ideal for that special hank of yarn you have been wanting to use. For the sample shown here I have used a gorgeous sparkly yarn.

MATERIALS

Hettestrikk Silver Sock (75% SW merino, 20% nylon, 5% silver stellina), 4ply, 400m (437½yd) in a 100g (3½oz) ball, in the following shade:

• Mulevika x 1 ball

3mm (US C/2 or D/3) crochet hook (or size required to match tension [gauge])

2 x easily removable different coloured markers (I'll be using green and blue markers)

Note that Hettestrikk dyes colourways to order, and Mulevika is the name of the colourway dyed for this batch.

TENSION (GAUGE)

After steam blocking: 2 pattern reps and 6 rounds measure 5 x 5cm (2 x 2in) over lace pattern worked in the round using a 3mm (US C/2 or D/3) hook.

When you are making your tension swatch make sure it is done in the round as tension can differ between working in rows and rounds.

FINISHED SIZE

Please note that measurements are after steam blocking and that the crochet fabric might stretch more lengthwise and widthwise with wet blocking.

Leg – measured from chainless foundation made when separating for heel, to top of cuff – 9cm (3½in) long. Note that crochet lace has a great stretch.

SOCK SIZE	M	L
Shoe size UK (US)	5-6 (7-8)	7-8 (9-10)
Foot circumference (approximate)	20cm (8in)	25cm (10in)
Foot length (approximate)	22cm (8¾in)	24cm (9½in)

Special Stitch

Fan: [2dc, ch1, 2dc] all in same st or sp.

Pattern Notes

These socks start from the toe. The lace pattern is worked on the foot. Space for the afterthought heel is created, then the lace continues on the leg, and a delicate chain edge is created on top. The afterthought heel is worked in single crochet.

There are only two sizes for the lace socks, but it is easy to adjust the size. For a smaller size, change the hook size, use 2.5mm hook and size M pattern. Work 2 fewer rounds on the foot for a shorter length or 2 or more rounds for a longer length, but please take into account that crochet lace stretches.

SOCKS (MAKE 2)

TOE

Using a 3mm (US C/2 or D/3) hook and A, ch15 (15).

Round 1: 3sc in 2nd ch from hook, place green marker in the centre sc of 3-sc group, 12sc, 3sc in next ch, place blue marker in the centre sc of 3-sc group, working into opposite side of foundation chain, 12sc. 30 (30) sts

Move markers up as you work.

Your new round will start 1 st before green marker.

Round 2: 2sc in next st, 1sc in st with green marker, 2sc in next st, 1sc in every st to 1 st before blue marker, 2sc in next st, 1sc in st with blue marker, 2sc in next st, 1sc in every st to 1 st before green marker. 34 (34) sts

Round 3: 1sc in every st to end.

Rep Rounds 2 and 3 a further 3 (6) times. 46 (58) sts

Next round: 2sc in next st, 1sc in st with green marker, 1sc in every st to blue marker, 1sc in st with blue marker, 2sc in next st, 1sc in every st to 1 st before green marker. 48 (60) sts

Next round: 1sc in every st to end, moving markers as you work.

FOOT

Set-up round: 1sc in next st and st with green marker, 2sc, the last st worked will now be the beg of round, skip next 2 sts, Fan in next st, skip next 2 sts, [1dc in next st, skip 2 sts, Fan in next st, skip next 2 sts] 7 (9) times, sl st into top of first st to join. 8 (10) Fans

All markers can now be removed. Continue to lace pattern.

LACE PATTERN

When instructed to work 'in next Fan', work the st(s) into the 2ch-sp of Fan. Skip all other sts of Fan.

Round 1: ch1 (does not count as a st here and throughout), 1sc in first st, ch2 (counts as 1dc here and throughout) 2dc in same st as last sc, 1sc in next Fan, [Fan in next sc, 1sc in next Fan] 7 (9) times, 2dc in first sc, sl st into top of beg 2 ch to join.

Round 2: ch1, 1sc in first st, Fan in next sc, [1sc in next Fan, Fan in next sc] 7 (9) times, sl st into first sc to join.

Rounds 1 and 2 form the Lace pattern.

Rep Lace pattern pattern a further 9 (10) times, then rep Round 1 once more. 19 (21) rounds worked in total.

CHART

The chart is read from right to left on every round.

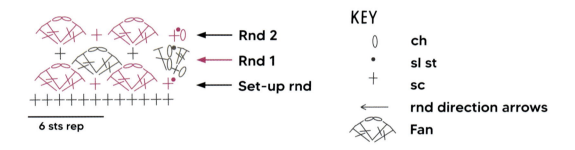

KEY

0	ch
•	sl st
+	sc
←	rnd direction arrows
〈Fan symbol〉	Fan

6 sts rep

Separating for heel

M size

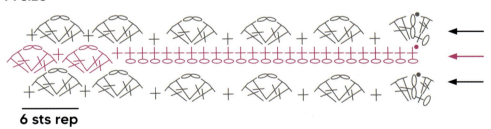

6 sts rep

L size

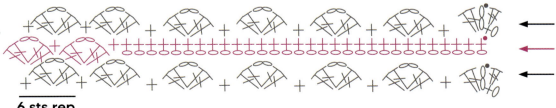

6 sts rep

SEPARATING FOR HEEL

Next round: Chainless foundation 24 (30) sc, skip next 3 (4) Fans, 1sc in next Fan, Fan in next sc, [1sc in next Fan, Fan in next sc] 3 (4) times, sl st to first st of chainless foundation to join.

Next round: Working into chainless foundation, ch1, 1sc in first st, ch2, 2dc in same st as last sc, skip 2 sts, 1sc in next st, skip 2 sts, [Fan in next sc, skip 2 sts, 1sc in next st, skip 2 sts] 4 (5) times, now working into sts of top of foot, [Fan in next sc, 1sc in next Fan] 4 (5) times 2dc in first sc, sl st into top of beg 2 ch to join. 8 (10) Fans

Starting with Round 2, rep Rounds 1 and 2 of Lace pattern 4 times, then rep Round 1 once more. 10 (10) (10) rounds worked in total from chainless foundation.

Edge: ch4, [1sc, ch5, 1sc] in next Fan, ch3, * 1sc in next sc, ch3, [1sc, ch5, 1sc] in next Fan, ch3; rep from * to end.

Fasten off.

AFTERTHOUGHT HEEL

Heel is worked in a continuous spiral. 2ch-sps are counted as a st.

With RS facing, join yarn with 1sc at the bottom right corner of heel opening. Working along the sole, ch1, 2sc in first st, 22 (28) sc across missed Fans and sts from separating for heel, 2sc in next st, place blue marker in last st made, working along the other side of chainless foundation, 2sc in first st, 22 (28) sc, 2sc in next st, place green marker in last st made. 52 (64) sts

Move markers up as you work.

Round 1: 1sc2tog, 1sc in every st to 2 sts before blue marker, 1sc2tog, 1sc in marked st, 1sc2tog, 1sc in every st to 2 sts before green marker, 1sc2tog, 1sc in marked st. 48 (60) sts

Round 2: 1sc in every st to end.

Round 3: 1sc2tog, 1sc in every st to 2 sts before blue marker, 1sc2tog, 1sc in st with marker, sc2tog, 1sc in every st to 2 sts before green marker, sc2tog, 1sc in st with marker. 44 (46) sts

Rep Rounds 2 and 3 a further 5 (5) times. 24 (26) sts.

Fasten off leaving a yarn tail of approximately 15cm (6in). Using tapestry needle and yarn tail, sew heel opening closed. Weave in the yarn end.

FINISHING

Weave in ends and block as preferred (see Finishing and Caring for Socks).

Crochet Fair Isle Allover Socks

Crochet Fair Isle provides a wonderful opportunity to experiment with colour. I have designed the colourwork chart for this project to be easily memorable as I wanted the enjoyment to come from the technique and colour play. There are also lots of 'rest' rounds, worked with just one colour, which give you a little break from the Fair Isle technique.

MATERIALS

John Arbon Textiles Exmoor Socks (60% Exmoor Blueface, 20% Corriedale, 10% Zwartbles, 10% nylon) 4ply, 200m (218¾yd) in 50g (1¾oz) skein (hank), in the following shade:

- A – Dimity x 1 skein (hank)
- B – Mizzle x 1 skein (hank)
- C – Aggy x 1 skein (hank)
- D – Blooth x 1 skein (hank)
- E – Fairy Thimble x 1 ball

3mm (US C/2 or D/3) crochet hook (or size required to match tension [gauge])

2 x easily removable different coloured markers (I'll be using green and blue markers)

TENSION (GAUGE)

After steam blocking: 12 sts and 10 rounds measure 5 x 5cm (2 x 2in) over scBLO in Fair Isle worked in the round using a 3mm (US C/2 or D/3) hook.

When you are making your tension swatch make sure it is done in the round as tension can differ between working in rows and rounds.

FINISHED SIZE

Please note that measurements are after steam blocking and that the crochet fabric might stretch more lengthwise and widthwise with wet blocking.

Leg – measured from top of heel to top of cuff – 17.5 (16) (14)cm/7 (6¼) (5½)in.

SOCK SIZE	S	M	L
Shoe size UK (US)	3-4 (5-6)	5-6 (7-8)	7-8 (9-10)
Foot circumference (approximate)	16.5cm (6½in)	18cm (7in)	19.5cm (7¾in)
Foot length (approximate)	20cm (8in)	23cm (9in)	24.5cm (9½in)

Pattern Note

Use sticky notes or washi tape to mark the round you are working on on the chart. This will you to keep track.

LEFT SOCK

TOE

Using 3mm (US C/2 or D/3) hook and yarn A, ch13 (13) (13).

Round 1: 1sc in 2nd ch from hook and in every ch across, rotate work 180 degrees and begin working into opposite side of foundation chain, sc in every st across, do not join. 24 (24) (24) sts

Round 2: 3 sc in first st (place green marker in centre sc of 3-sc group), 11sc, 3sc in next st (place blue marker in centre sc of 3-sc group), 11sc. 28 (28) (28) sts

Move markers up as you work.

Round 3: 1sc in every st to end.

Round 4: 1sc in every st to green marker, 3sc in marked st (moving marker up to middle sc of 3-sc group just made), 1sc in every to blue marker, 3sc in marked st (moving marker up to middle sc of 3-sc group just made), 1sc in every st to end. 32 (32) (32) sts

Round 5: 1sc in every st to end.

Rep Rounds 4 and 5 a further 1 (2) (3) times, then rep Round 4 once more. 40 (44) (48) sts

FOOT

The blue marker can now be removed. Change colour on stitch with green marker, keep this marker in place to denote the beginning of round.

Work from chart using the Fair Isle technique.

Each square of chart represents one stitch and each stitch is worked in scBLO.

The chart is read from right to left on every round.

Work in a continuous spiral, do not join round with sl st or ch1 at the beg of round.

Change colour by working the last st of round until you have 2 loops on hook, drop old colour and pick up new one, finish the st with new colour.

Do not fasten off yarn on every round, carry it with you up as you work catching it every other round.

Catch yarn every other stitch to avoid creating big loops.

Starting with stitch 1, work the 4-st pattern rep 10 (11) (12) times per round.

Work Rounds 1 to 12 of chart twice, then work Round 25 as follows:

Round 25: Using yarn B, * [2scBLO in next st] twice, 18 (20) (22) sc; rep from * once more. 44 (48) (52) sts

Continue to work from chart until you have completed Round 28 (32) (36). The foot is now complete.

Continue to heel and leg.

HEEL

The heel is worked in rows over half the number of stitches and starts with Round 29 (33) (37) of chart.

Using yarn A.

Keep marker in place to ensure you work the heel in the correct position relative to the toe. **

Row 1 (RS): 22 (24) (26) scBLO, turn.

Row 2 (WS): ch1, 1sc in every st to 1 st from end of row, leave last st unworked, turn. 21 (23) (25) sts

Rep row 2 a further 11 (11) (13) times, ending with WS facing for next row. 10 (12) (12) sts for next row

Next row (WS): ch1, 1sc in every st to end, 1sc in side of row below, 1sl st in skipped st from row below, turn. 11 (13) (13) sts

Next row (RS): ch1, skip 1sl st, 1sc in

every st to end, 1sc in side of last row, 1sl st in skipped st from row below, turn. 12 (14) (14) sts

Rep last row a further 10 (12) (14) times, do not turn after last row. 22 (24) (26) sts

Join in colour E (B) (B) in last sl st.

Work in scBLO to marked stitch.

The heel should be parallel to the toe.

LEG: SIZE S ONLY

Work Rounds 30 to 37 of chart.

SIZE M ONLY

Work Rounds 34 to 37 of chart.

ALL SIZES

Rep Rounds 2 to 12 of chart once, rep the 4-st pattern 11 (12) (13) times around.

Next round: Using yarn B, * [2scBLO in next st] twice, 18 (20) (22) sc; rep from * once more. 48 (52) (56) sts

Rounds 26–37: Cont to work from chart.

Fasten off all yarns and join yarn A.

CUFF

The cuff is worked back and forth in rows in scBLO, and joined to the last round of sock with sl sts.

Ch8 (8) (8).

Row 1 (RS): 1sc in second ch from hook, 1sc in every ch to end, skip next st of last round of sock, sl st in next st, turn. 7 (7) (7) sts

Row 2: ch1, 1scBLO in every st to end, turn.

Row 3: ch1, 1scBLO in every st to end, skip st with sl st and next st of last round of sock, sl st in next st, turn.

Row 4: ch1, 1scBLO in every st to end, turn.

Rep Rows 3 and 4 until the rib has been worked all around the top of sock.

Join last row of rib to first row by sl st across row, working into back of beg chains of Row 1 and BLO of last row of rib.

Fasten off.

FINISHING

Weave in ends and block as preferred (see Finishing and Caring for Socks).

RIGHT SOCK

Work as for right sock to **

Row 1 (RS): With B, ch1, 22 (24) (26) scBLO, change to yarn A, 22 (24) (26) scBLO, turn.

You will only work on stitches in yarn A for the heel.

Work remainder of Right sock as for left sock.

CHART

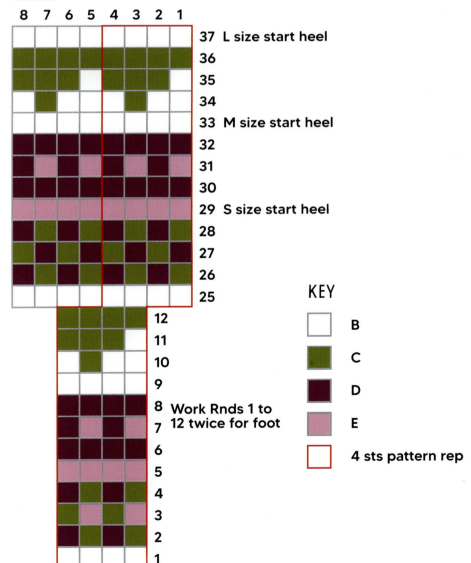

37 L size start heel
36
35
34
33 M size start heel
32
31
30
29 S size start heel
28
27
26
25

12
11
10
9
8 Work Rnds 1 to
7 12 twice for foot
6
5
4
3
2
1

KEY

B	(white)
C	(green)
D	(dark)
E	(pink)

4 sts pattern rep

Shortie Socks

These very comfortable socks are perfect to wear as slippers. You may wish to apply non-slip glue to the sole and heel to prevent them from slipping. If you wish to wear them in shoes, choose yarn with 25% nylon for longevity.

MATERIALS

West Yorkshire Spinners The Croft DK (100% Shetland Islands wool), DK, 225m (246yd) in 100g (3½oz) skein (hank) in the following shades:

- A – Harkland (226) x 1 skein (hank)
- B – Tangwick (1021) x 1 skein (hank)

3.5mm (US E/4) crochet hook (or size required to match tension [gauge])

2 x easily removable different coloured markers (I'll be using green and blue markers)

TENSION (GAUGE)

After steam blocking: 10 sts and 9 rounds measure 5 x 5cm (2 x 2in) over scBLO worked in the round using a 3.5mm (US E/4) hook.

When you are making your tension swatch make sure it is done in the round as tension can differ between working in rows and rounds.

FINISHED SIZE

Please note that measurements are after steam blocking and that the crochet fabric might stretch more lengthwise and widthwise with wet blocking.

Leg – measured from top of heel to top of cuff – 4cm (1½in) long.

SOCK SIZE	S	M	L
Shoe size UK (US)	3-4 (5-6)	5-6 (7-8)	7-8 (9-10)
Foot circumference (approximate)	20cm (8in)	22cm (8¾in)	24cm (9½in)
Foot length (approximate)	21cm (8¼in)	23cm (9in)	25cm (10in)

Pattern Note

Single crochet in the back loop creates a fabric with ample stretch; however if you want the socks to be looser, use a 4mm (US G/6) crochet hook.

SOCKS (MAKE 2)

TOE

Using 3.5mm (US E/4) hook and yarn A, ch 11 (11) (11).

Round 1 (RS): 1sc in 2nd ch from hook and in every ch across, rotate to work into opposite side of foundation chain, 1sc in every ch across, do not join round. 20 (20) (20) sts

Round 2: 3sc in first st (place green marker in centre sc of 3-sc group), 9sc, 3sc in next st (place blue marker in centre sc of 3-sc group), 9sc. 24 (24) (24) sts

Move markers up as you work.

Round 3: 1sc in every st to end.

Round 4: 1sc in every st to green marker, 3sc in marked st, moving marker up to middle sc of 3-sc group just made, 1sc in every st to next marker, 3sc in marked st moving marker up to middle sc of 3-sc group just made, 1sc in every st to end. 28 (28) (28) sts

Round 5: 1sc in every st to end.

Rep Rounds 4 and 5 a further 2 (3) (4) times. 36 (40) (44) sts

FOOT

The blue marker can now be removed, keeping only the green marker in place to denote the beginning of round.

Work in scBLO in a continuous spiral, moving marker up as you work, for 21 rounds or until sock measures 12.5 (13.5) (14.5)cm/5 (5¼) (5¾)in. Change to B and fasten off A.

Next round: [2scBLO in next st, 17 (19) (21) scBLO] twice. 38 (42) (46) sts

Work 3 rounds in scBLO.

Next round: [2scBLO in next st, 18 (20) (22) scBLO] twice. 40 (44) (48) sts

Work in scBLO in a continuous spiral, moving marker up as you work, until sock measures 17 (17.5) (18.5)cm/6¾ (7) (7¼)in

HEEL

Heel is worked in rows over half of the total number of stitches.

Row 1 (RS): ch1, 20 (22) (24) scBLO, change to yarn B, 20 (22) (24) scBLO, turn.

You will now work in sc using yarn B only for the heel.

Row 2 (WS): ch1, 19 (21) (23) sc, leave last st unworked, turn. 19 (21) (23) sts

Row 3: ch1, 18 (20) (22) sc, leave last st unworked, turn. 18 (20) (22) sts

Row 4: ch1, 1sc in every st to 1 st before end, leave rem st unworked, turn. 17 (19) (21) sts

Rep Row 4 a further 7 (9) (9) times. 10 (10) (12) sts

Next row (WS): ch1, 1sc in every st to end, 1sc in side of row below, 1sl st in skipped st from row below, turn. 11 (11) (13) sts

Next row (RS): ch1, skip sl st, 1sc in every st to end, 1sc in side of row below, sl st in skipped st from row below, turn. 12 (12) (14) sts

Rep last row a further 8 (10) (12) times. 20 (22) (24) sts

Join yarn A with sl st in last sl st of heel (the one made in last skipped st). This should be on the same side as the marker. Fasten off yarn B.

LEG

Work 5 rounds in scBLO.

Next round: [1sc2togBLO, 18 (20) (22) scBLO] twice, 1sc2tog, 1sc in every st to end. 38 (42) (46) sts

Change to yarn B and fasten off yarn A.

Rounds 1 to 4: 1scFLO in every st to end.

Fasten off and roll the top edge outwards.

FINISHING

Weave in ends and block as preferred (see Finishing and Caring for Socks).

Moss Stitch Socks

These socks are ideal slipper socks to wear around the house or in wide shoes, such as rubber clogs. The toe up design is easy to work and the moss stitch adds plenty of charm.

MATERIALS

Rico Superba Alpaca Luxury Socks (62% virgin wool, 23% polyamide, 15% alpaca), sport, 310m (339yd) in a 100g (3½oz) ball, in the following shade:

• Silver Grey (004) x 1 ball

3.5mm (US E/4) crochet hook (or size required to match tension [gauge])

2 x easily removable different coloured markers (I'll be using green and blue markers)

TENSION (GAUGE)

After steam blocking: 9 sts and 10 rounds measure 5 x 5cm (2 x 2in) over pattern (1scBLO, 1csc) worked in the round using a 3.5mm (US E/4) hook.

When you are making your tension swatch make sure it is done in the round as tension can differ between working in rows and rounds.

FINISHED SIZE

Please note that measurements are after steam blocking and the crochet fabric will stretch more lengthwise and widthwise with wet blocking.

Leg – measured from top of heel to top of picot edge – 6cm (2½in) in length.

SOCK SIZE	S	M	L
Shoe size UK (US)	3–4 (5–6)	5–6 (7–8)	7–8 (9–10)
Foot circumference (approximate)	21cm (8¼in)	23.5cm (9¼in)	25.5cm (10in)
Foot length (approximate)	21cm (8¼in)	22cm (8¾in)	23cm (9in)

Pattern Notes

The sock is made in a continuous spiral.

The yarn used for this project is quite fluffy, which means the finished socks are a lot wider. If you would like a tighter fit, choose a smooth DK yarn as a substitute.

You may wish to apply non-slip glue to the sole and heel to prevent them from slipping.

SOCKS (MAKE 2)

TOE

Using a 3.5mm (US E/4) hook, ch12 (12) (12).

Round 1: 1sc in 2nd ch from hook and in each ch across, rotate work 180 degrees and beg working into opposite side of foundation chain, 1sc in each st across, do not sl st to join round. 22 (22) (22) sts

Round 2: 3sc in first st (place green marker in centre sc of 3-sc group), 10sc, 3sc in next st (place blue marker in centre sc of 3-sc group), 10sc. 26 (26) (26) sts

Move markers up as you work. Green marker denotes beg of round.

Round 3: 1sc in each st to end.

Round 4: 3sc in marked st, move green marker up to middle sc of 3-sc group just made, 1sc in each st to blue marker, 3 sc in marked st, move marker up to middle sc of 3-sc group just made, 1sc in each st to end. 30 (30) (30) sts

Rep Rounds 3 and 4 a further 2 (3) (4) times. 38 (42) (46) sts

Remove blue marker. Keep green marker in place to denote the beg of round, moving it up as you work.

Next round: 1scBLO loosely in each st to end, 1scBLO in marked st.

FOOT

Round 1: [1csc, 1scBLO] to end.

Round 2: [1scBLO, 1csc] to end.

Rounds 1 and 2 form the moss stitch pattern. Work in pattern until piece measures 16 (17) (18)cm/6¼ (6¾) (7)in ending with Round 1 of pattern.

SEPARATING FOR HEEL

Round 1: Chainless foundation 19 (21) (23) sc, skip next 19 (21) (23) sts, 1scBLO, [1csc, 1scBLO] to end.

Round 2: 19 (21) (23) sc, 1csc, [1scBLO, 1csc] to end. 38 (42) (46) sts

Rounds 3 to 10: Starting with Round 1 of moss stitch pattern, work in pattern for 8 rounds.

EDGE

Next round: [1sc2tog, 17 (19) (21) sc] twice, sl st in first st to join. 36 (40) (44) sts

Next Round: ch1, 1sc in first st, picot, * 2sc, picot; rep from * to last st, 1sc, sl st in first st to join.

AFTERTHOUGHT HEEL

The heel is worked in a continuous spiral. Extra stitches are worked around the heel opening to help prevent any holes at the point where you separated for the heel.

With RS facing, join yarn with 1sc at the bottom right corner of heel opening. Working along the sole, 19 (21) (23) sc, 1sc in gap in between stitches in corner, place blue marker on last st made. Working along the other side of opening (the leg part), 19 (21) (23) sc, 1sc in gap in between stitches in corner, place green marker in last st. 40 (44) (48) sts

Round 1: 1sc2tog, 1sc in every st to 2 sts before blue marker, 1sc2tog, 1sc in marked st, 1sc2tog, 1sc in every st to 2 sts before green marker, 1sc2tog, 1sc in marked st. 36 (40) (44) sts

Move markers up as you work.

Round 2: 1sc in each st to end.

Rep Rounds 1 and 2 a further 3 (3) (3) times. 24 (28) (32) sts

Rep Round 1 once more. 20 (24) (28) sts

Fasten off leaving a tail of approximately 15cm (6in). Using a tapestry needle and yarn tail, sew heel opening closed. Weave in the yarn end.

FINISHING

Weave in ends and block as preferred (see Finishing and Caring for Socks).

Stripy Socks

Stripes always produce a fun fabric and these socks are super quick to make. The stripes are created in half double crochet worked in the third loop, which results in a very interesting effect , where the top of the stitches face forwards. It's even more effective when changing colour.

MATERIALS

Birdstreet Yarn (75% superwash merino, 25% nylon), DK, 225m (246yd) in a 100g (3½oz) ball, in the following shades:

- A – Medici x 1 skein (hank)

Birdstreet Yarn (75% superwash merino, 25% nylon), DK, 425m (464 ¾yd) in a 100g (3½oz) skein (hank), in the following shades:

- B - Roll Over Pavlova x 1 ball

3.5mm (US E/4) crochet hook (or size required to match tension [gauge])

3 x easily removable different coloured markers (I'll be using green, blue and yellow markers)

TENSION (GAUGE)

After steam blocking: 11hdc3L and 10 rounds measure 8 x 8cm (3 x 3in) over hdc3L worked in the round using a 3.5mm (US E/4) hook (or size required to match tension [gauge]). When you are making your tension swatch make sure it is worked in the round as tension can differ between working in rows and rounds.

FINISHED SIZE

Please note that measurements are after steam blocking and the crochet fabric will stretch more lengthwise and widthwise with wet blocking.

Leg – measured from top of heel to top of cuff – 13cm (5in) in length.

SOCK SIZE	S	M	L
Shoe size UK (US)	3-4 (5-6)	5-6 (7-8)	7-8 (9-10)
Foot circumference (approximate)	17cm (6¾in)	19cm (7½in)	20cm (8in)
Foot length (approximate)	19.5cm (7¾in)	22cm (8¾in)	23.5cm (9¼in)

Pattern Note

These socks have a cuff down construction, with heel flap. The hdc3L stitch produces a beautiful and stretchy fabric; however, if you would like the socks to be bigger use a 4mm (US G/6) crochet hook.

Special Stitch

Half double crochet in third loop (hdc3L): *hdc creates 3 loops in a st, one at the front, and two at the back; when working into third back loop of every st, work into the very last loop, right at the back of the stitch.*

RIGHT SOCK

CUFF

Using a 3.5mm (US E/4) hook and yarn A, ch8 (8) (8).

Row 1: 1sc in 2nd ch from hook, 1sc in every ch to end, turn. 7 (7) (7) sts

Row 2: ch1 (does not count as a st here and throughout), 1scBLO in every st to end, turn.

Rep row 2 a further 34 (36) (38) times, ending with WS facing for next row.

SEAM CUFF

Hold first and last rows together and, working in BLO of sts of both rows, ch1, sl st across to join. Do not fasten off.

LEG

Rotate piece to work in row-ends of cuff.

Round 1: ch1, 36 (40) (44) hdc evenly spaced around top edge of cuff. Do not join.

Place yellow marker in first st for beginning of round and move marker up as you work.

Continue to work hdc3L in a continuous spiral.

Change to yarn B.

Round 2: Hdc3L in every st to end.

Change to yarn A.

Round 3: As Round 2.

Rep Rounds 2 and 3 changing colour as set 6 more times, then work Round 2 once more (16 rounds worked in total). **

HEEL FLAP

The heel is worked in yarn A, back and forth in rows and sc over half the sock, leaving the rem (top of the foot) sts unworked.

Row 1 (RS): 18 (20) (22) sc in 3L, turn, leaving rem sts unworked.

Row 2 (WS): ch1, 1sc in every st to end of row, turn. 18 (20) (22) sts

Rep Row 2 a further 12 (14) (16) times. Total of 14 (16) (18) rows worked for the heel flap.

TURN THE HEEL

Row 1 (RS): ch1, 9 (10) (11) sc, 1sc2tog, 1sc in next st, leave rem sts unworked, turn. 11 (12) (13) sts

Row 2: ch1, 2sc, 1sc2tog, 1sc in next st, turn. 4 (4) (4) sts

Row 3: ch1, 1sc in every st to 1 st from end of row, 1sc2tog working the first half of the st in the next st and the second half into the next st 2 rows below, 1sc, turn.

Rep Row 3 a further 5 (5) (7) more times. 10 (10) (10) sts

SIZE M ONLY

Next row: ch1, 1sc in every st to 1 st from end of row, 1sc2tog working the first half of the st in the next st and the second half into the next st 2 rows below, turn.

Rep last row once more. - (10) (-) sts

All the unworked stitches have been used up and you have turned your heel. 10 (10) (12) sts

ALL SIZES: GUSSET

Round 1 (RS): ch1, 10 (10) (12) sc, 7 (8) (9) sc evenly along edge of heel flap (working 1 st in every other row, approx.), place green marker on last st made, 18 (20) (22) hdc3L (across sts of foot), 7 (8) (9) sc evenly along edge of heel flap, place blue marker on first st made. 42 (46) (52) sts

You are now at the end of the round.

Start working in a continuous spiral, changing colour as set for stripes.

Move all markers up as you work.

Change to yarn B.

Round 2: 1hdc in every st to 2 sts before green marker, 1hdc2tog, 1hdc in marked st, 1hdc3L in every st to blue marker, 1hdc in marked st, 1hdc2tog, 1hdc in every st to end. 40 (44) (50) sts

Change to yarn A.

Round 3: 1hdc3L in every st to end, moving marker up as you work.

Change to yarn B.

Round 4: 1hdc3L in every st to 2 sts before green marker, hdc3L2tog, hdc3L in marked st, hdc3L in every st to blue marker, hdc3L in marked st, hdc3L2tog, hdc3L in every st to end. 38 (42) (48) sts

Rep Rounds 3 and 4 a further 1 (1) (2) times. 36 (40) (44) sts

FOOT

Keep only the blue marker in place, move it up on every round and work in hdc3L in a continuous spiral, changing colour as set, until work measures 15.5 (17) (18.5)cm/6 (6¾) (7¼)in from the back of the heel, ending with a stripe in B and at blue marker.

TOE

Fasten off yarn B and continue with A.

Set-up round: 1sc in 3L in marked st, 17 (19) (21) sc in 3L, 1sc in 3L in next st, place green marker in st just made,17 (19) (21) sc in 3L, 1sc in st with blue marker.

Move markers up as you work. The blue marker denotes beg of round.

Round 1: 1sc2tog, 1sc in every st to 2 sts before green marker, 1sc2tog, 1sc in marked st, 1sc2tog, 1sc in every st to 2 sts before blue marker, 1sc2tog, 1sc in marked st. 32 (36) (40) sts

Round 2: 1sc in every st to end.

Round 3: 1sc2tog, 1sc in every st to 2 sts before green marker, 1sc2tog, 1sc in marked st, 1sc2tog, 1sc in every st to 2 sts before blue marker, 1sc2tog, 1sc in marked st. 28 (32) (36) sts

Rep Rounds 2 and 3 a further 3 (3) (3) times. 16 (20) (24) sts

Fasten off leaving a yarn tail of approximately 15cm (6in). Thread tail onto a tapestry needle and sew the toe opening closed. Weave in the yarn end.

FINISHING

Weave in ends and block as preferred (see Finishing and Caring for Socks).

LEFT SOCK

Work as for Right sock to **.

Fasten off yarn B.

HEEL FLAP

The heel is worked in yarn A, back and forth in rows of sc over half the sock, leaving the rem (top of the foot) sts unworked.

Row 1 (RS): Skip the next 18 (20) (22) sts and join A with an sc in 3L of next st, 18 (20) (22) sc in 3L, turn. You will work across the first 18 (20) (22) sts only for the heel flap.

Row 2 (WS): ch1, 18 (20) (22) sc, turn.

Rep Row 2 a further 12 (14) (16) times. Total of 14 (16) (18) rows worked for the heel flap.

Work remainder of Left sock as for Right sock.

Overlay Mosaic Cube Socks

The overlay mosaic crochet technique is used here as it was in the the Simple Overlay Crochet Socks, but this pattern is more advanced. The playful cube design provides ample opportunity for you to play with colour. Self striping yarn was used in this example but two solid colours with high contrast would also be beautiful.

MATERIALS

West Yorkshire Spinners Signature 4ply (75% wool, 25% nylon), 4ply, 400m (437½yd) in a 100g (3½oz) ball, in the following shade:

• A – Dusty Miller 0129 x 1 ball

Rico Ricorumi Neon Sock (75% wool and 25% polyamide), 4ply, 400m (437½yd) in a 100g (3½oz) ball, in the following shade:

• B – Neon Pink 002 x 1 ball

3mm (US C/2 or D/3) hook (or size required to match tension [gauge])

2 x easily removable different coloured markers (I'll be using green and blue markers)

TENSION (GAUGE)

After steam blocking: 12 sts and 12 rounds measure 5 x 5cm (2 x 2in) in overlay mosaic pattern worked in the round using a 3mm (US C/2 or D/3) crochet hook.

When you are making your tension swatch make sure it is done in the round as tension can differ between working in rows and rounds.

FINISHED SIZE

Please note that measurements are after steam blocking and the crochet fabric will stretch more lengthwise and widthwise with wet blocking.

Leg – measured from chainless foundation made when separating for heel, to top of cuff – 11cm (4¼in) in length

SOCK SIZE	S	M	L
Shoe size UK (US)	3–4 (5–6)	5–6 (7–8)	7–8 (9–10)
Foot circumference (approximate)	16cm (6¼in)	18.5cm (7¼in)	21cm (8¼in)
Foot length (approximate)	21cm (8¼in)	23cm (9in)	25cm (10in)

Pattern Note

These socks have good stretch due to the scBLO and FLdc2d stitches, however, no increases are placed around the heel. If you would like smaller or larger socks, add or take away 6 stitches to the toe. This is the length of pattern repeat and it should measure around 2.5cm (1in).

Special Stitch

Front loop double crochet 2 down (FLdc2d):
Working in front of sts from previous row, work a double crochet in FLO of st 2 rows below.

SOCKS (MAKE 2)

TOE

Using 3mm (US C/2 or D/3) hook and yarn A, ch13 (13) (13)

Round 1: 1sc in 2nd ch from hook and every ch across, working into opposite side of foundation chain, 12 (12) (12) sc across, do not join. 24 (24) (24) sts

Round 2: 3sc in first st, place green marker in centre sc of 3-sc group, 11 (11) (11) sc, 3sc in next st, place blue marker in centre sc of 3-sc group), 11sc. 28 (28) (28) sts

Move markers up as you work.

Round 3: 1sc in every st to end.

Round 4: 1sc in every st to first marker, 3sc in marked st moving marker up to middle sc of 3-sc group just made, sc in every st to next marker, 3sc in marked st moving marker up to middle sc of 3-sc group just made, sc in every st to end. 32 (32) (32) sts

Rep Rounds 4 and 5 a further 2 (4) (5) times. 40 (48) (52) sts.

SIZE S AND L ONLY

Next round: As Round 3.

Next round: 1sc in every st to first marker, 2sc in marked st moving marker to first of 2 sts just made, 1sc in every st to next marker, 2sc in marked st, remove marker, 1sc in every st to end. 42 (–) (54) sts

Foot and leg are worked in a continuous spiral, place green marker to denote the beg of round.

OVERLAY MOSAIC SECTION

Instructions for chart are written and charted, please follow whichever you are more comfortable with.

FOOT

Round 1 (RS): Using yarn B, 1scBLO in every st to end.

Round 2: Using yarn A, 1scBLO in every st to end.

Round 3: Using yarn B, * [1scBLO, FLdc2d] twice, 2scBLO; rep from * to end.

Round 4: Using yarn A, * FLdc2d, 3scBLO, FLdc2d, 1scBLO; rep from * to end.

Round 5: Using yarn B, * 5scBLO, FLdc2d; rep from * to end.

Round 6: Using yarn A, * FLdc2d, 3scBLO, FLdc2d, 1scBLO; rep from * to end.

Round 7: Using yarn B, * [1scBLO, FLdc2d] twice, 2scBLO; rep from * to end.

Round 8: Using yarn A, 2scBLO, FLdc2d, 3scBLO; rep from * to end.

Round 9: Using yarn B, * [1scBLO, FLdc2d] twice, 2scBLO; rep from * to end.

Rep Rounds 3 to 8 a further 4 (4) (5) times, then rep Rounds 3 and 4 once more.

CHART

Change colour on every round by working to last st of round, stop when there are 2 loops on hook, finish off the stitch with new colour.

Do not fasten off colour on every round but carry it with you up the side and use when needed.

Join yarn B and work in overlay mosaic technique, changing colour on every round.

Work from chart using scBLO and mosaic dc.

The chart is read from right to left on every round.

The column marked with 0 is a colour indicator column. Do not include this column in the pattern repeat.

Starting with Round 1, work from chart A repeating Rounds 3 to 8 a total of 5 (5) (6) times, then rep Rounds 3 and 4 once more.

CHART A

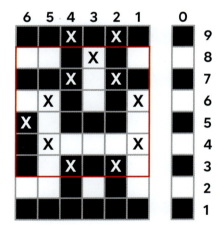

KEY

☐ **Yarn A**

■ **Yarn B**

☐ **6 sts pattern rep**

X **FLdc2d**

SEPARATING FOR HEEL CHARTS

Work from a Chart – choose the correct one for your size.
Using A, chainless foundation 21 (24) (27) sc, skip next 21 (24)
(27) sts, rep pattern to end.

Starting with Round 6 of Chart A, work Rounds 6 to 8 once,
then Rounds 3 to 8 three times, then work Round 9 once.

CHART B: SIZE S

CHART B: SIZE M

CHART B: SIZE L

SEPARATING FOR HEEL

Next round: Using yarn A, working from Round 5 of Chart B (for your size), chainless foundation 21 (24) (27) sc, skip next 21 (24) (27), rep mosaic pattern to end.

Starting with Round 6 of Chart A or written instructions, working in overlay mosaic crochet, rep Rounds 3 to 8 a total of 4 (4) (4) times, then work Round 9.

Fasten off yarn A, continue with yarn B.

CUFF

Cuff is worked back and forth in rows in back loop single crochet, and joined to the last round of sock with sl sts. 9 (9) (9) ch.

Row 1 (RS): 1sc in second ch from hook, 1sc in every ch to end, skip next st of last round of sock, sl st in next st, turn. 8 (8) (8) sts

Row 2: ch1 (does not count as a st), 1scBLO in every st to end, turn.

Row 3: ch1, 1scBLO in every st to end, skip st with sl st and next st of last round of sock, sl st in next st, turn.

Row 4: ch1, 1scBLO in every st to end, turn.

Rep Rows 3 and 4 until the rib has been worked all around the top of sock.

Join last row of rib to first row by sl st across row, working into back of beg chains of Row 1 and BLO of last row of rib.

Fasten off.

AFTERTHOUGHT HEEL

Heel is worked in a continuous spiral. Note that extra stitches are worked around the heel opening to help prevent any holes at the point where you separated for the heel.

With RS facing, join yarn A with 1sc at the bottom right corner of heel opening. Working along the sole, make 21 (24) (27) sc, 1sc in gap in between sts in corner, place blue marker on last st made. Working along the other side of opening (the leg part), 21 (24) (27) sc, 1sc in gap in between sts in corner, place green marker in last st made. 44 (50) (56) sts

Round 1: 1sc2tog, 1sc in every st to 2 sts before blue marker, 1sc2tog, 1sc in marked st, 1sc2tog, 1sc in every st to 2 sts before green marker, 1sc2tog, 1sc in marked st. 40 (46) (50) sts

Move markers up as you work.

Round 2: 1sc in every st to end.

Rep Rounds 1 and 2 a further 5 (6) (7) times, ending last rep with Round 1. 20 (22) (22) sts

Fasten off leaving a yarn tail of approximately 15cm (6in). Using a tapestry needle and yarn tail, sew heel opening closed. Weave in the end.

FINISHING

Weave in ends and block as preferred (see Finishing and Caring for Socks).

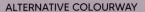

ALTERNATIVE COLOURWAY

MATERIALS

West Yorkshire Spinners Signature 4ply (75% wool, 25% nylon), 4ply, 400m (437½yd) in a 100g (3½oz) ball, in the following shades:

- A – Rum Paradise 822 x 1 ball
- B – Fuchsia 1002 x 1 ball

CROCHET STITCHES

Whether you're new to crochet or a more experienced crocheter who needs a reminder of how to work some of the stitches, this useful section contains all you need to complete the projects in this book.

SLIP KNOT

1. Loop the yarn as shown. (1)

2. Insert the hook into the loop, catch the yarn with the hook, and pull it through to make a loop over the hook. (2)

3. Gently pull the yarn to tighten the loop around the hook and complete the slip knot. (3)

CHAIN STITCH (CH)

Wrap the yarn over the hook and pull it through the loop on the hook to form a new loop on the hook. (4)

FOUNDATION CHAIN

Follow the instructions for making a chain to complete the first chain stitch. Repeat this process, drawing a new loop of yarn through the loop already on the hook until the chain is the required length. Count each V-shaped loop on the front of the chain as one chain stitch, except for the loop on the hook, which is not counted. (5)

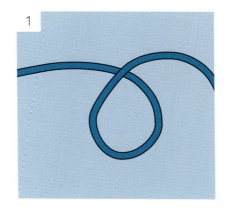

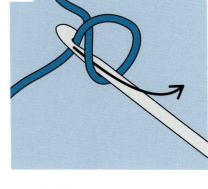

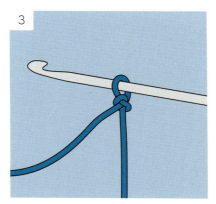

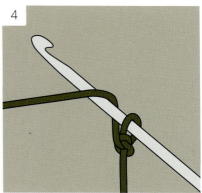

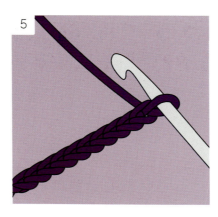

Tip

When making a foundation chain, after every few stitches, move up the thumb and finger that are grasping the chain to keep the chain stitches even.

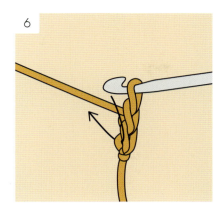

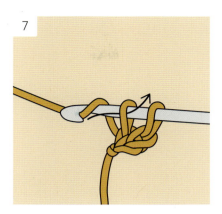

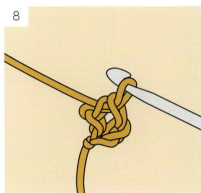

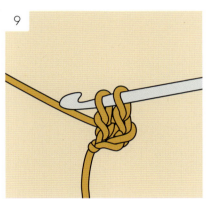

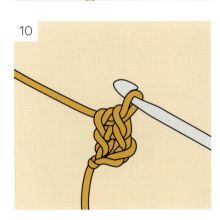

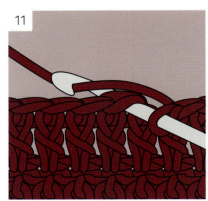

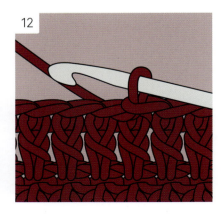

CHAINLESS FOUNDATION

A chainless foundation provides a stretchy, narrow edge which does not pull in and provides a ready-made row of single crochet. It a perfect start for top down socks and for creating stitches when you are separating for an afterthought heel.

1. Start with 2 chains, turn your work on the side, you will see a bump at the back of your chains (6). Insert your hook into the bump of the second chain from the hook.

2. Yo and pull yarn through the bump. You now have 2 loops on the hook (7). Yo again and pull through 1 loop only on the hook. You now have 2 loops on the hook. Yo and pull through both loops. That's the first stitch made (8)

3. To work the next stitch, turn your work on its side and you will see the front leg of the next stitch to be worked. Insert the hook into the front and back leg of the stitch (the full V)(9). Yo and pull it through the stitch, so that you have 2 loops on your hook.

4. Yo and pull through 1 loop, leaving 2 loops on the hook, then yo again, and pull through both loops on the hook. The second stitch is made. (10)

Rep steps 1 to 4 until you have the desired number of chainless foundation sc.

Tip

If you have never tried chainless foundation, I recommend practising with chunky yarn and a large hook, so that you will can the stitches. Work the beginning chains loosely.

SLIP STITCH (SL ST)

This stitch has no height; it is used to join rounds or to move to a different starting point for the next round or row.

1. Insert the hook into the stitch from front to back, yarn over. (11)

2. Pull the yarn through the stitch and through the loop on the hook. (12)

SINGLE CROCHET (SC)

A short stitch that creates a dense fabric.

1. Insert hook into a stitch or chain. (1). Yarn over and pull through the stitch/chain (two loops on the hook).

2. Yarn over again and pull through both loops on the hook (2) to finish the stitch. (3)

Rep steps 1 to 3 to create multiple single crochet stitches.

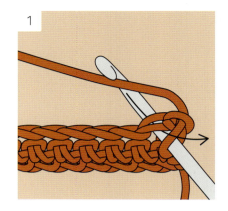

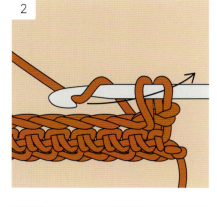

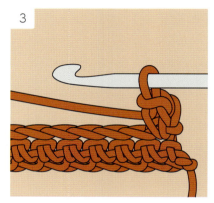

SINGLE CROCHET BACK LOOP/FRONT LOOP ONLY (SCBLO/FLO)

These stitches are worked just like the basic sc but into the back or front loop of a stitch and not the full stitch.

This results in a stretchy stitch that produces a fabric with a lot of give. It also does not slant, which makes it ideal for colour work. These stitches are used in several of the socks, in this book.

Tip

When working single crochet into a foundation chain, the chains can sometimes stretch, to prevent that work into the back bumps of the chain.

BLO

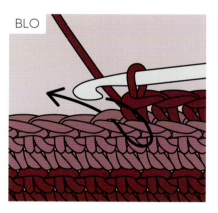

FLO

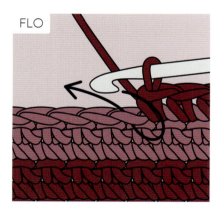

EXTENDED SINGLE CROCHET (ESC)

One of my favourite stitches to use in socks, also one of the most underrated stitches in crochet. This stitch has the height of half double crochet, but none of the looseness, It has a great stretch but also great structure.

1. Insert hook into next st, yo, pull up a loop (2 loops on hook). (4)

2. Yo and pull through one loop on hook only (2 loops on hook).

3. Yo and pull through both loops on hook. (5)

Rep steps 1 to 3 to create extended single crochet stitches.

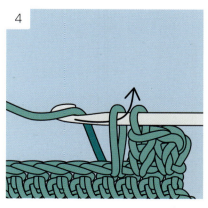

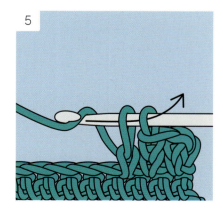

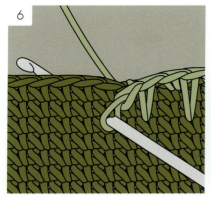

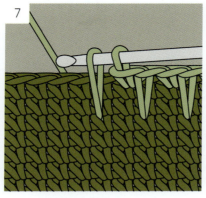

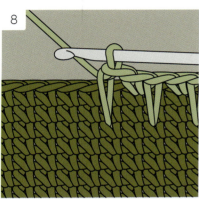

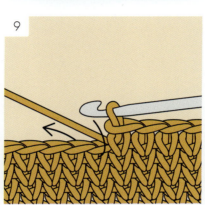

SPIKE SINGLE CROCHET (SSC)

1. Insert hook in round below (as instructed). (6)

2. Yo, pull loop through and up to the height of current row. (7)

3. Yo, pull through both loops on hook. (8)

Rep steps 1 to 3 to create spike single stitches.

CENTRE SINGLE CROCHET (CSC)

This stitch is also known as centre stitch or as 'knit stitch', as it looks like knitted stocking stitch. The only difference from working a standard single crochet is that you work waistcoat stitch into the body of the stitch, in between the strands (the V) of the front stitch and not into the top V as you usually do. The secret to success with centre sc is to keep a relaxed tension. Don't pull your stitches too tight as you will have to work into them on the next round. It also helps to use a pointy hook.

This stitch is perfect for colour work as it produces a smooth finish. It is also a very decorative stitch; however, it does have the tendency to create a tight fabric. Working this stitch loosely will result in more stretch to the crochet item and will also help when working the stitch.

Insert hook through the centre of the indicated stitch (between the V on the front of work, not the top) (9), yo, pull up a loop, two loops on your hook. Yo, draw through both loops on hook.

Rep steps 1 and 2 to create centre single crochet stitches.

HALF DOUBLE CROCHET (HDC)

This is a slightly taller stitch than single crochet, similar in height to extended single crochet, but, it does not posess the same structure. This stitch has great stretch, but it can be slightly too loose, which can give the fabric a 'gappy' look.

1. Yarn over and insert the hook into the stitch or chain. (1)

2. Yarn over and pull up a loop (three loops on hook). Yarn over again and pull through the three loops on the hook to finish the stitch. (2)

Rep steps 1 to 2 to create half double crochet stitches.

THIRD LOOP HALF DOUBLE CROCHET

(HDC3L)

Half double crochet creates three loops in a stitch, two at the front and one at the back. When instructed to work into the third loop of the stitch, work into the very last loop, right at the back of the stitch. (3 and 4)

DOUBLE CROCHET (DC)

This is a tall stitch that creates a more open fabric, which makes it unsuitable for the foot or leg parts of the socks. However, it is a perfect stitch to use in crochet lace, it creates beautiful fans, which you will find on the lace socks.

1. Yo and insert hook into stitch or chain. (5)

2. Yo and pull up a loop, (three loops on hook). (6)

3. Yo and pull through the first two loops on the hook (two loops on the hook). (7)

4. Yo and pull through the remaining two loops on the hook to finish the stitch. (8)

Rep steps 1 to 4 to create double crochet stitches.

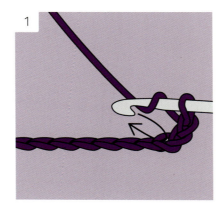
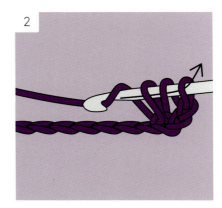
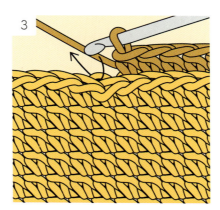
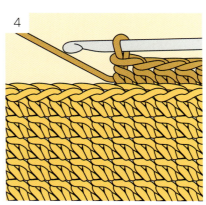
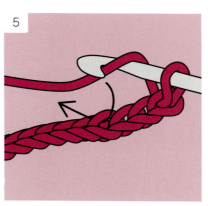
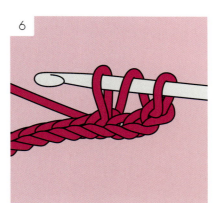
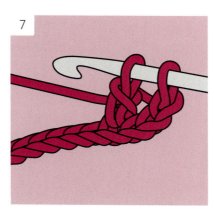
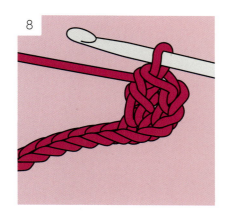

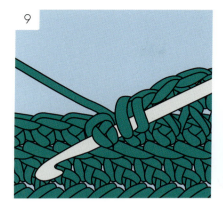

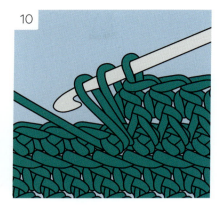

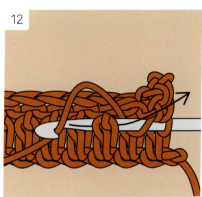

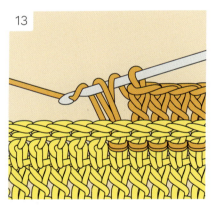

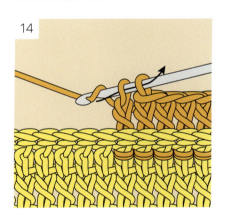

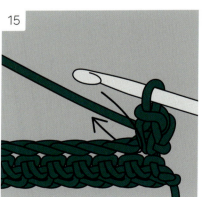

FRONT POST HALF DOUBLE CROCHET (FPHDC)

Yo, insert hook around post of next st from front to back to front again. (9) Yo, pull up a loop, yo, pull through all 3 loops on hook. (10)

FRONT POST DOUBLE CROCHET (FPDC)

1. Yo, insert hook around the post of next st from front to back to front again. (11)

2. Yo, pull up a loop, [yo, pull through 2 loops on hook] twice. (12)

BACK POST DOUBLE CROCHET (BPDC)

1. Yo, insert hook around the post of next st from back to front to back again. (13)

2. Yo, pull up a loop, [yo, pull through 2 loops on hook] twice. (14)

FPdc stitches are raised on the right side of the work and in relief on the wrong side, while BPdc stitches are raised on the wrong side and in relief on the right side

INCREASE

This method increases by one stitch. The illustrations show two single crochet worked into one stitch but the principle is the same when increasing using other stitches.

Work a single crochet as usual into the next stitch, then work a second single crochet into the same stitch. (15)

Tip

The invisible increase is an alternative to a standard increase: work the first stitch in the front loop and the second stitch in both loops of the same stitch.

DECREASE SINGLE CROCHET (SC2TOG)

This method decreases by one stitch. The illustrations show single crochet two stitches together (sc2tog), but the same principle is used when decreasing other stitches.

1. Insert the hook in the next stitch, yo and pull a loop through the stitch (2 loops on the hook). (1)

2. Insert the hook in the second stitch, yo and pull a loop through the stitch (3 loops on the hook). Yo and pull through all 3 loops on the hook. (2)

EXTENDED SINGLE CROCHET 2 TOGETHER (ESC2TOG)

1. (Insert hook in next st, yo and pull up a loop, yo and pull through 1 loop only) twice. (3)

2. Yo and draw through all 3 loops on hook. (4)

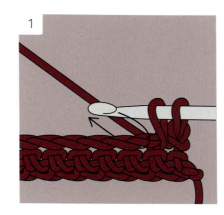
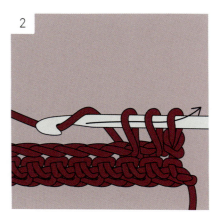
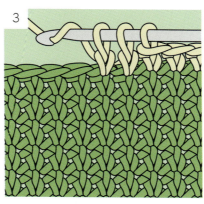
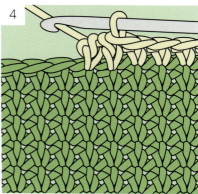

OTHER TECHNIQUES

This section contains more advanced techniques; from cables to Fair Isle, they are fantastic techniques that are fun to make and add a lot of interest to your project.

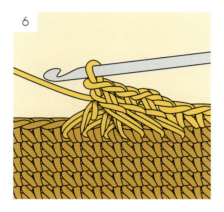

Tip

When working back on the twisted stitches make sure to work each of the six cable stitches – some of them can hide behind those at the front.

CABLES

Cables create a textured fabric with lots of visual interest. This method for creating cables involves using front post double crochet, meaning you will only work the cables into the front post of stitches. Cables are made by skipping a set of stitches, then working back into their posts by crossing front post stitches to create the twists.

In the cable socks project, I have used cable 6 front (c6F) cables and placed them in a bed of centre single crochet on each side to make them stand out a little bit more.

1. Skip next 3 sts, 3FPdc in next sts. (5)

2. Working in front of the sts just made, 3FPdc in skipped sts. (6)

3. Next round: you will work FPdc in the stitches with the cable, making sure that you work every stitch of the 6 cable stitches, the twist can cause the stitches to hide behind the front ones, so check carefully. (7)

FAIR ISLE CROCHET

Fair Isle crochet is worked into the back loop of every stitch because this prevents your work from slanting, meaning the colour pattern looks better. The Fair Isle Pine Tree socks are worked in centre single crochet; however, the colour changes are worked in exactly the same way as for scBLO.

To achieve a neat colour change, you need to change colours one stitch before. For example, if the third stitch needs to be a different colour, change yarns on the last stage of the second stitch.

1. Work to one stitch before the colour change, stop the last stitch when you have two loops on the hook. (1)

2. Drop colour A and finish the stitch with colour B. (2)

3. Work in colour B until you need to go back to colour A on the next stitch, finish the last stitch of colour B with colour A, ready for next stitch. (3 and 4)

Continue repeating steps 1 to 3 while following the chart.

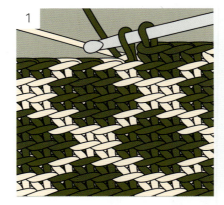
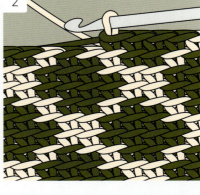
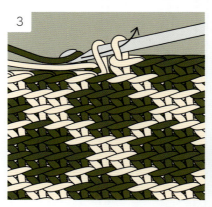
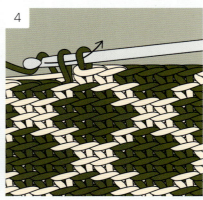

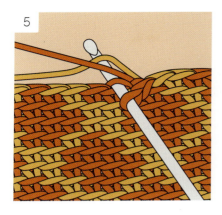

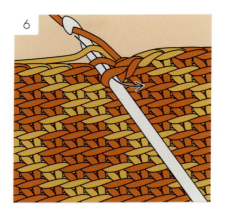

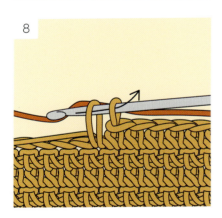

Tip

When working with two yarn colours per row, keep one colour to your left and one to your right and do not twist them. This will prevent the yarn from tangling.

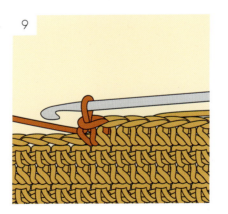

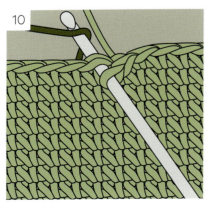

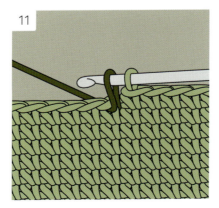

CARRYING YARN

When working Fair Isle crochet you will need to carry both yarn colours with you throughout, and only use them when necessary. When one yarn colour is not in use for a few stitches, it needs to be stranded. The neatest way to do this is to catch the yarn every other stitch when not in use. Therefore, always carry the yarn at the back of the work and strand when necessary, this results in neat and lovely colour work.

1. When inserting the hook to work the next scBLO make sure that the yarn to be stranded is placed on top of the hook at the back of work. (5)

2. Work scBLO as usual, enclosing the strand in the stitch. (6) Continue repeating these two steps, enclosing the yarn not in use every second stitch. Image 7 shows the reverse of the fabric.

CHANGING COLOUR

METHOD 1

Change colour by working the last st of the round until you have two loops on the hook, drop the old colour and pick up the new one, finish the stitch with the new colour. (8 and 9)

METHOD 2

This colour change happens when you are joining a round with a sl st at the end.

Simply insert your hook into first stitch to join the round, place the new colour on the hook and finish the sl st with the new colour. (10 and 11)

JOIN YARN

To join in a new colour or new yarn, simply work to the last stage of the stitch, and when you have two loops on hook, place the new colour on the hook and finish the stitch with new colour.

FRONT LOOP DOUBLE CROCHET 2 DOWN

(FLDC2D)

1. Yo, insert hook into the front loop into corresponding stitch two rows below. (1)

2. Yo and pull up a loop (three loops on hook). (2)

3. Yo and pull through two loops only, yo and pull through remaining two loops. (3)

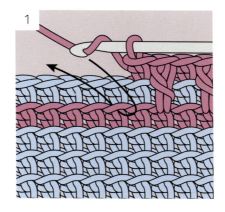

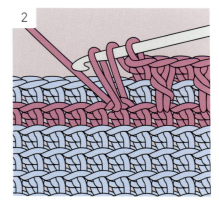

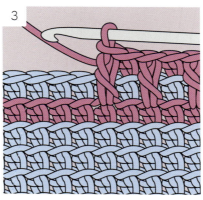

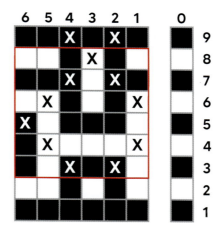

Tip

Your FLdc2d will always need to be worked into the first round below of the same colour.

OVERLAY MOSAIC CROCHET

This is a colour work technique that allows you to create a beautiful pattern using just one colour per round.

You will work single crochet in the back loop only (BLO), and place front loop double crochet two rows down (FLdc2d) when required, working FLdc2d into the front loops of the stitches from the first row below of the same colour. You will notice in the chart that dark/dark and light/light squares have the letter X. This stands for FLdc2d and is a clear indication of where the front loop double crochet needs to be worked.

The round numbers are only on the right-hand side because you will only work on the right side of the work in the round.

The chart is read from right to left on every round.

The column marked with 0 is a colour indicator column. This shows which colour you will use on each round. Do not include this column in the pattern repeat.

KEY

⬜	**Yarn A**
⬛	**Yarn B**
🟥	**6 sts pattern rep**
X	**FLdc2d**
0	**Colour indicator column**

SAMPLE CHART

JOINING

The openings on afterthought heels, and the toes on top down socks need to sewn up to complete the socks. Choose a stitch that does not result in a bulky and hard seam as this will rub on your toes or heel.

Start by turning your sock inside out so that the WS is facing.

When you are seaming toes and afterthought heels, fold the sock flat, making sure the heel is centred at the back of the foot. Hold the two sides of the opening as you work.

WHIP STITCH

One seaming method is whip stitch; however unlike the standard way of working this stitch, you will work in both loops of the stitch using a tapestry needle.

Hold the two sides of the opening together. Work a line of diagonal stitches from back to front under the two strands of each stitch at the edges of the panels. (4)

SLIP STITCH SEAM

Work a row of slip stitches through both top loops of the stitches on each panel. (5)

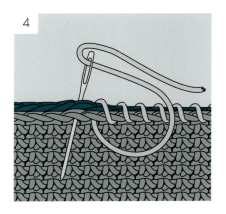

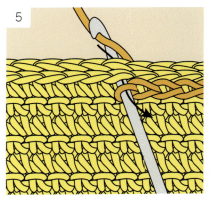

TENSION (GAUGE)

Tension (gauge in the US) is the number of stitches (or pattern repeats) and rounds (or rows) to a given measurement, usually 2.5, 5 or 10cm (1, 2 or 4in). For your work to be the correct size, the tension specified in the pattern must be matched as closely as possible. Tension not only depends on hook and yarn, but also on personal technique. Just because a pattern recommends a certain hook size does not necessarily mean that your tension will be the same, which is why it is vital to always make a swatch and measure the tension before you start your project.

MEASURING TENSION

As socks are worked in the round, the tension swatch needs to be in the round as well, because the tension may differ when worked in rows. All tension in this book is measured over 5cm (2in), so work a piece of crochet larger than 5 x 5cm (2 x 2in), around 10 x 10cm (4 x 4in) is ideal. This will give you enough space to correctly count the stitches and rows. Lay the swatch on a flat surface, and use a tape measure and pins to mark out the desired size over which the gauge needs to be measured. Count exactly how many stitches and rows are within this square. (6) If you have more stitches or rows, this means you are a tight crocheter, so increase your hook size. If you have fewer stitches or rows, this means you are a loose crocheter, so go down a hook size.

Tip

All the toes or heel openings have been seamed using whip stitch, purely because it's softer and less bulky. However, do experiment with joining methods.

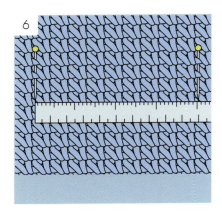

FINISHING & AFTERCARE

The final stage of any crochet make is blocking. This stage sets the stitches and gives you the chance to shape the socks. There are also a few simple things you can do to look after your socks once you've finished them.

BLOCKING

When you have finished your socks, it is recommended that you block them to even out your tension (gauge) and so that the stitches will smooth out.

There are two blocking methods: steam blocking and wet blocking. Steam blocking is my personal favourite, and this is the method I have used for every sock in this book.

TOOLS FOR BLOCKING

I favour rust resistant, T-shaped metal pins for blocking, although most pins will do; just make sure they do not have plastic tops (when steam blocking) and are rust resistant.

You'll also need a towel or ironing board, steam iron (for steam blocking only) and a flat surface.

STEAM BLOCKING

Cover a flat surface with a towel. Place your socks on the towel and pin them in place, without stretching. DO NOT stretch out the ribbing.

Steam lightly, holding the iron 2.5cm (1in) above the fabric. Allow the steam to penetrate for several seconds.

Allow the project to dry before taking out the pins.

WET BLOCKING

Fill a basin or bowl with cold or lukewarm water, you may wish to add a small amount of detergent, such as wool wash. Leave the socks to soak for 10 to 15 minutes. Do not agitate them otherwise they might felt or shrink.

Remove the socks from the water without stretching them, and at the same time squeeze the excess water out, (do not wring the item).

Lay the socks on a dry towel and roll, loosely applying pressure to remove excess water.

Pin the socks out without stretching them on a dry, flat surface. Alternatively place them on sock blockers.

Allow to dry naturally. Make sure the socks are completely dry before removing pins or before removing from sock blockers.

CARING FOR SOCKS

You do not need to wash crochet socks after every wear because wool is breathable and odour resistant, but this of course depends on whether they are actually dirty and how you feel about rewearing items.

How you wash your socks will depend on the washing instructions on the yarn label. If the yarn is not superwash the sock should be washed by hand. If the yarn is superwash, they can be washed in the washing machine; however, I would always recommend the wool cycle with the lowest spin.

STORING SOCKS

Clothes moths are the enemy of handmade items, and it is vital to store your socks correctly to avoid the little pesky yarn eaters. The perfect way is to add cedar blocks or lavender pouches to the drawer where the socks are stored. They are inexpensive and easily available. You can also store your socks in cotton bags.

When storing your socks you must make sure that the socks are washed and fully dried. Making sure there is no moisture in them at all as wool can rot in damp conditions, not to mention that this kind of environment is ideal for moths to thrive.

Fold your socks or roll them like a swiss roll, but do not pull the cuff over the ball as this will permanently stretch the cuff.

ABOUT THE AUTHOR

Anna Nikipirowicz is a crochet and knit designer, tutor, and author. Her designs are regularly featured in craft magazines such as *Inside Crochet* and she is the author of *Mosaic Chart Directory for Knitting and Crochet*, *Tunisian Crochet Stitch Dictionary*, *Crocheted Wreaths for the Home*, and more.

Find her on her website www.moochka.co.uk and @annanikipirowicz on Instagram or @MoochkaUK on Facebook.

ACKNOWLEDGMENTS

My biggest thank you is to my amazing husband, Dave, whose constant love, support and belief in me spurs me on. To my cats, Ollie and Brick who are the most reliable yarn checkers.

Thanks to Sarah, Jess, Lindsay and the fantastic team at David and Charles for making this book a reality. Thanks also to Jason, the photographer, for the stunning photos in this book.

Thank you to the amazing Sharon for tech editing. And thank you to all of you, for purchasing the book and loving crochet socks.

SUPPLIERS

WEST YORKSHIRE SPINNERS
www.wyspinners.com

RICO DESIGN
www.rico-design.de/en/home

JOHN ARBON TEXTILES
www.jarbon.com

HETTESTRIKK
www.hettestrikk.no

LANG YARNS
www.langyarns.com

BIRDSTREET YARN
www.birdstreet.com

HJERTGARN
www.hjertgarn.dk

ROWAN YARN
www.knitrowan.com

SANDNES GARN
www.sandnesgarn.no

INDEX

A DAVID AND CHARLES BOOK
© David and Charles, Ltd 2025

David and Charles is an imprint of David and Charles, Ltd
Suite A, Tourism House, Pynes Hill, Exeter, EX2 5WS

Text and Designs © Anna Nikipirowicz 2025
Layout and Photography © David and Charles, Ltd 2025

First published in the UK and USA in 2025

ISBN-13: 9781446314517 paperback
ISBN-13: 9781446314531 EPUB

This book has been printed on paper from approved suppliers and made from pulp from sustainable sources.

MIX
Paper | Supporting responsible forestry
FSC® C136333

Printed in China through Asia Pacific Offset for:
David and Charles, Ltd
Suite A, Tourism House, Pynes Hill, Exeter, EX2 5WS

10 9 8 7 6 5 4 3 2 1

Publishing Director: Ame Verso
Senior Commissioning Editor: Sarah Callard
Publishing Manager: Jeni Chown
Editor: Jessica Cropper
Tech Editor: Sharon Carter
Project Editor: Lindsay Kaubi
Lead Designer: Sam Staddon
Designers: Blanche Williams and Jess Pearson
Pre-press Designer: Susan Reansbury
Illustrations: Kuo Kang Chen
Art Direction: Sarah Rowntree
Photography: Jason Jenkins
Production Manager: Beverley Richardson

David and Charles publishes high-quality books on a wide range of subjects. For more information visit www.davidandcharles.com.

Share your makes with us on social media using #dandcbooks and follow us on Facebook and Instagram by searching for @dandcbooks.

Layout of the digital edition of this book may vary depending on reader hardware and display settings.